# A FACE BESIDE THE FIRE
# MEMORIES OF
# DAWN GREY OWL-RICHARDSON

By

## Bob Richardson

To Pat & Verda
Best Wishes
Bob Richardson

Steller's Jay Art and Publishing
Bob Richardson
2-1951 Lodgepole Drive,
Kamloops, BC. V1S 1Y1
EMAIL: robert_richardson@telus.net
or phone 250-374-3237

**National Library of Canada Cataloguing in Publication Data**

Richardson, Bob, 1928-
A face beside the fire

Includes bibliographical references.
ISBN 1-55212-719-2

1. Grey Owl, Dawn. 2. Richardson, Bob, 1928- 3.
Naturalists--Canada--Biography. I. Title.
QH31.G74R52 2001        508'.092        C2001-910571-1

# TRAFFORD

**This book was published** *on-demand* **in cooperation with Trafford Publishing.**
On-demand publishing is a unique process and service of making a book available for retail sale to the public taking advantage of on-demand manufacturing and Internet marketing.
**On-demand publishing** includes promotions, retail sales, manufacturing, order fulfilment, accounting and collecting royalties on behalf of the author.

Suite 6E, 2333 Government St., Victoria, B.C. V8T 4P4, CANADA

| | | | |
|---|---|---|---|
| Phone | 250-383-6864 | Toll-free | 1-888-232-4444 (Canada & US) |
| Fax | 250-383-6804 | E-mail | sales@trafford.com |
| Web site | www.trafford.com | TRAFFORD PUBLISHING IS A DIVISION OF TRAFFORD HOLDINGS LTD. |
| Trafford Catalogue #01-0118 | | www.trafford.com/robots/01-0118.html |

10    9    8    7    6    5    4    3

# DEDICATION

to
Sandra, Glaze & Grey
and
To All My Children

Anahareo receiving The Order of Canada by Governor General Edward Schruyer 1983, along with Anahareo's grandson Glaze.
Photo courtesy Kamloops Daily News

Little Dawn at Lake Ajawaan
Photo courtesy collection of the Grey Owl family personal collection. 1930's

Mountain home built by Bob & Dawn 1978-1979

Dawn's daughter Sandra

# 1
## Prologue

Archie Belaney, who became known as Grey Owl, was born in Hastings, England September, 1888. His mother Kitty Belaney, formerly Kitty Cox, was only fourteen years of age when little Archie was born. Because of Kitty's unfortunate marriage to George Belaney, his two spinster sisters, Ada and Carrie raised young Archie until he became seventeen years of age.

His upbringing in typical Victorian England was that of firm hands by both of his aunts, insisting that he grow up to be a well-educated gentleman and fit in to society as they believed he should. Archie was educated in the Hastings Grammar School, and was also given lessons in classical piano.

During his youth, Archie was always fascinated with dreams of animal life and the wilderness of North American Indians. He was determined to see and meet the Aboriginal people of North America, and to learn their language, their ways and customs.

Archie arrived in Canada when he was seventeen years of age and found his way to the Temagami area of Ontario, and eventually to the Bear Island Indian Reservation. He was taken in and accepted by the people of Bear Island, taught their language as well as their ways of trapping and hunting. With his basic education in England he became a spokes person for many Aboriginal people.

After meeting Gertrude Bernard in the Temagami area in the mid 1920`s, he married this very attractive young Mohawk. She abhored the killing of animals and eventually changed Archie`s course of life from trapper to conservationist. He lectured across United States, throughout Eastern Canada and the United Kingdom. He even entertained the Royal Family in Buckingham Palace.

Gertie was also known as Anahareo, and she and Archie had a daughter whom they named Dawn. Dawn was my late wife and, she too became a torch bearer for her parents and their philosophy of respect for our Great Canadian Wilderness.

*FOREWORD*

*No one kept the name of Grey Owl alive in the 1960`s and 1970`s more than his daughter Dawn. All her adult life she defended her father as did her mother, Anahareo, from those who underscored his contribution to the cause of conservation. She knew how timely his central message was: "You belong to Nature, not it to you".*

*In his book her husband Bob Richardson sensitively recounts the years of their relationship: their first meeting, marriage, and life together. In many ways it reads like a modern version of "Pilgrims of the Wild", Grey Owl's own account of his life with Anahareo, the story of a growing relationship.*

*Bob describes Dawn's tremendous personal strength in the face of poor health. At the age of nine she became seriously diabetic. For the first time it tells of Dawn's discovery in 1976 of Leonard Scott-Brown, her father's half-brother, then living in Vancouver, who became a second father to her. It recounts interesting stories of Dawn's and Bob's search of the meaning of Grey Owl and Anahareo, through trips to places where they lived in northern Canada in the late 1920s and early 1930s.*

*Dawn helped me enormously over a fifteen year period with the preparation of my biography of her father, "From the Land of Shadows" (1990). Unfortunately she did not live to see it in print, as she died six years before it appeared. I loved reading Bob's account as it brought her back to life for me, this warm, intelligent, fun-loving woman, who recognized the enormous contribution of both her father and mother to conservation, and wanted the world to know it as well.*

*Donald Smith, Ph.D*
*Professor of History, University of Calgary*

Chapter 1

I noticed a single tear trickle down Dawn's cheek, as we passed the Kamloops City Limits sign at 90 klicks, heading North on the Yellowhead beginning our journey to Quebec. I knew it was a tear of joy. We were finally going to see Lake Simon in Northern Quebec to view the exact spot where, in 1926, Chief Papati had performed the marriage ceremony for Dawn's parents, Grey Owl and Anahareo.She had been looking forward to visiting some of these spots for a long time.

It was early July, 1983. Sunshine warmed our hearts as we journeyed through mountains and across the Prairies. After four days of travelling, Dawn and I stopped for a three-day visit with my relatives in Thunder Bay, Ontario.

On the North shore of Lake Superior, Thunder Bay snuggles itself tightly to the Pre Cambrian Shield. As we drove into town at dusk, we saw the lighthouse flashing on the tip of Nanabijou, welcoming us as it has greeted thousands of ships to the Great Lakes Port, the gateway to the West, for more than a hundred years.

When we arrived at the Village of Lake Simon two weeks later, I approached an elderly Indian sunning himself on his front porch, for directions to the lake.

And now, as I read Dawn's diary entry of our travels, it nourishes my soul:

*"We passed the church, turned left down a sandy road, and Lake Simon came into full view. We saw a red canoe coming towards us at great speed, paddled by two young Indian boys. We stood on a board-walk watching. Bob took a photo, then he walked down to the shore of the lake. I followed the board-walk that stretched along the high bank above the sandy beach. As I walked along alone, I saw an old wooden dock that protruded out into the water. I visualized a canoe being pulled up on shore by a tall, thin man, smiling as he did so at a dark-skinned young Indian girl, with almond-shaped eyes, sitting in the canoe. The man held out his hand to her and, at the moment their fingers touched, the picture disappeared; my throat burned and I started to cry. It was the closest moment I have ever had to both of my parents at the same time. I felt an overwhelming joy because I was at Lake Simon."*

Sharing my life with Dawn began in 1973. I was living alone in a small travel trailer parked in a local campground in Kamloops. At this point in my life, I had been a Rail Traffic Controller for CN for twenty-eight years. The trailer didn't have room for my avocation painting Canadian land-scapes. Over the years I had been doing a lot of painting, and I not only needed a place to show my work, but also a studio to work in.

One evening I was walking alone along West Victoria Street and came to the old CPR Office building that had been boarded up for a long time. I noticed it had been cleaned up and opened as an Artisans studio. Upon entering the front entrance, I was greeted by a short, plump gentleman, almost bald and with a big smile and glistening blue eyes, who greeted me warmly. I noticed one man doing leather work, and another gentleman whittling small wood carvings.

My welcome guide was the man who leased the building. He was enthusiastic about the project, although selective about who he rented space to. Each unit rented for $50.00 per month. As long as the artisan renting an eight by ten booth was conscientious, ready to devote a few hours daily to help make the whole project a success, the hours for attending were flexible. There was still a window unit available for a visual artist, and the gallery organizer hoped who ever rented it would add credibility to his over-all business project. The next day I took several of my oils for his viewing, and he told me I was welcome and invited me to rent space and set up to join the group.

It was the beginning of a new and exciting adventure; one like I had never experienced before. I felt great and pleased with a new lifestyle of painting during my free evening hours.

At 4:00p.m. each day, I left my office with CN and went directly to my new and exciting locale as a painter.

Within a week of the facility opening, people became interested in the variety of activities taking place there. Some would walk amongst the booths and browse, and others would stand outside and watch me. My unit's window faced the main street, so I often had an audience as I worked on my landscapes.

Inside the front entrance to the right was a large glass showcase with jewellery, precious rock artefacts and numerous other gift shop items. Behind the glass case was a cash register and small counter where the creator of the gallery and his wife, handled all sales for the artists for a ten percent commission. We were pleased with the business umbrella and felt it was a great opportunity for all who participated. We were happy to co-operate in such a project.

A few days after I had set up my painting booth, a young lady who appeared to be of Aboriginal background took over the last remaining booth on the premises. I watched as she and her daughter stocked her shelves with books, and arranged numerous photographs on her front counter.

I found the lady very attractive and she stirred my senses, and I wanted to introduce myself. She was slender, about five-foot-five tall, her black hair was done up in a French roll and her sparkling brown eyes attracted me. I had already decided I would introduce myself to her when there was an appropriately quiet time.

A couple of days later, I visited her gallery, noticing the titles on the books she had available: *"Pilgrims of The Wild...Men of the Last Frontier...Tales of an Empty Cabin, and The Adventures of Sajo and The Beaver People. "*

My thoughts regressed to my days of youth when I had been aware of the phrase " *Pilgrims of The Wild*". I repeated over and over again in my mind until finally the name of Grey Owl surfaced. I stood by her counter and looked over the photographs she had neatly displayed. She came over, and in a soft and gentle voice spoke: *"My name is Dawn.*"

I immediately knew who she was, and who her world-famous parents were. I was speaking with the daughter of Grey Owl and Anahareo. I knew about her parents including the fact they were the first Environmental  Conservationists hired by Parks Canada early in the 1930`s

*"My name is Bob,"* I replied, attracted by her quiet, unassuming and soft manner.  She interested me greatly, and I felt I really wanted to know more about her. I particularly wanted to know if she was free and uncommitted to anyone. I wasn`t aware at the time, that this meeting would be the beginning of  a strong feeling between us.

My daily job as a Rail Traffic Controller for CN  had been negatively affecting me. Controlling train traffic on the single-track line between Kamloops and Vancouver,

was at times nerve wrecking. Through the winter months
and on into spring, avalanches and rock slides
were a common occurrence. With the task of setting
meetings points for all the train traffic, we were also
required to dispatch patrolmen on velocipedes not more
than 25 minutes ahead of all trains through the Fraser
Canyon. The Canyon, at times, was a treacherous piece
of track and it had claimed a number of lives over the
years. Some trains had been wiped off the rails with the
engine and crew meeting their fate in the Fraser River far
below.

Yet it was only after meeting and visiting with Dawn that
I began to feel good and confident, ready to meet each
day and the duties I had to perform. It seemed to provide
a therapy of balance in my life that I so badly needed at
the time, and it allowed me hope and  to feel good about
myself.

A few evenings after our introduction, Dawn suggested
that after the 9:00p.m. closure of the gallery, we go out for
a lunch together. We went to The Golden Dragon
restaurant on our first evening out. Together we had two
glasses of wine each and a feast of Chinese food.  I found
Dawn very easy to be with and enjoyed the unpretentious
conversation. We sat and talked and talked, until the
waitress announced that since it was 1:00a.m. in the
morning the restaurant would like to close.

It seemed we were drawn together in some predermined

force. I believe both of us realized almost immediately there was a good possibility of a future together; a new phase of life.

One of Dawn`s girl friends had a ladies` wear store on the north side of town, and after our initial outing at the Golden Dragon we would frequently visit Margie, the owner, after gallery closing. In fact we went two or three evenings each week to visit with Margie, who lived in quarters at the back of the store. We would share a bottle or two of wine and an enjoyable visit. I was four years older than Dawn, and Margie was several years older than me. She and Dawn clicked merrily as friends.

The three of us began spending social times together. After a glass or two of wine, we would frequently saunter down one block to the local North Shore Steak and Pizza House. Then I`d try to be back to my trailer by midnight, as except for Saturdays and Sundays, my day shift with CN started early each morning.

A fellow who also worked in my CN office had made several vacation trips to the Malaga, Spain area of the Mediterranean Coast. His stories of Spain inspired me to want to travel there, and to take Dawn with me. The more I thought about it the more I thought it was a great idea. "Let`s go to Spain", I remarked to Dawn. " We could ride a donkey across Spain. That way we`d meet the common people," I stated. I must have persisted too hard while trying to talk Dawn into such a commitment. Earlier she had warned me not to push my luck, not to try and arrange her life. As I kept persisting she told me in no uncertain terms, that I could go to Spain and ride a donkey all by myself. I sat myself back in the chair quickly for a cooling of the atmosphere.

After her annoyance passed and things became calm again, I looked her right in the eye and said: *"I'm going to give you a new nickname. I will introduce you to all of my friends as, 'Little Big Mouth!"* That must have been our first flare of temper. Dawn broke into laughter and the nickname continued to amuse us for the rest of her life.

I still look back upon our first burst of temper with a chuckle. I did learn though, not to press my wishes and expectations too firmly. I learned that we made decisions through quiet discussion shared between the two of us.

As I continued to go straight to the gallery following my CN shift finishing at 4:00p.m., we got to know each other that summer. On the weekends, we would take part of the day for a country drive. Dawn's daughter, Sandra, a tall slim girl with black hair, and many of her mother's pleasant features, frequently took care of the booth so Dawn and I could go out. Dawn's six-foot-two son, Glaze, was slim and had blue eyes like his grandfather, Grey Owl, also took his turn at tending to his mother's business. That gave Dawn and I more time alone.

Sometimes we would drive to Wells Grey Park and walk the cedar-lined pathways to Dawson Falls. The huge cedars and spruce towered seventy feet above us, shading the bright sun. We returned often, and Dawn talked about her father and her regrets about the forest her father had never seen; he had never travelled to British Columbia.

She spoke eloquently and often about her father, and how some people failed to see his foresight about protecting the future of our great wilderness areas. He had influenced Dawn, and all who listened, that these areas depended upon humanity for protection for future generations to come. He drew attention to the greed for economic gain, that over-trapping along with the massive destruction of our forests would be devastating for future generations.

Dawn was dedicated to her parents' vision of environmental destruction taking place in our great country of Canada. She was proud of her parents vision, and was often invited to speak to school children, and at Winter Festivals to which she was frequently invited.

She talked about trying to curb the trapping methods which had changed very little over the past four-hundred years. Dawn felt the wolf had been designated as a vicious killer, because of the negative myths and fairy tales like *"Little Red Ridinghood."*

I understood and supported her dedication to her own as well as her parent's belief. I saw her soft diplomacy when speaking to people about Grey Owl and Anahareo. Because of my own upbringing in rural North-Western

**13**

Ontario, and being a young hunter and trapper myself in the 1930's, when she spoke about the massive killing of animals, along with the destruction of forests, I experienced the depth of her feelings. I had, myself, lived the lifestyle of rural bush people, much the same as Grey Owl had lived during his first years in Canada prior to his meeting Anahareo. I had been a kid trapper and wood-cutter living in Ontario, only two-hundred miles from the Temagami area where Grey Owl was located. I shared and fully understood the pain of her feelings.

Despite the complexities of her parents' history, Dawn was always understanding and compassionate to questions. I often listened enthralled to the manner in which she spoke and answered people, and felt it was an honour just to be by her side.

Sometimes we would drive to Savona, half-an-hour west of Kamloops to visit my friends. There we would sit around a bonfire with a drink of brandy, or a glass of their home-made wine, and sing songs into the late hours of the night. Looking back on our beautiful times together, and the summer of 1973, we got to know each other well as we shared our special times.

We also did very well from a business point of view during that summer in the artisans gallery. Dawn sold many copies of her father's books and her mother's Best Seller book, *Devil In Deerskins*. As well, I sold a lot of paintings. That summer passed too quickly considering our camp-fire social life and the rewarding results from our work.

In September, I knew I was ready to move from my travel-trailer. Sharing the washrooms with the travelling tourists no longer worked for me. I started looking for better living arrangements, and when I checked the local newspaper I discovered an appealing apartment on the North shore. That same evening I made a deposit on a two-bedroom suite. I could move in October 1st. For the rest of September I took a room in the old Franklin Hotel, conveniently located just one block from the Gallery. That increased my work time at the gallery and also the time I was able to be with Dawn.

The following Saturday afternoon in the Gallery, I noticed two men meandering throughout the premises. They were taking photographs. I had a feeling trouble was brewing, but was mystified what the problem could be. Something was up! I spoke with the Leather Maker who was also feeling suspicious about the peculiar activities taking place. When we closed that evening and I discussed with Dawn what I thought could be a problem, she was nervous. She not only had a large supply of books on consignment from the publisher, but also many personal irreplaceable historical photographs of her family.

Sunday afternoon we learned what the problem was. Foreclosure loomed ahead. I loaded all of Dawn`s books in my car and we took them to her apartment. Then I returned to the Gallery and repeated the process with all of my paintings. We had to get out of there, I felt. Monday morning, a padlock was placed on all of the doors.

On October 1st, I moved into my rented apartment. The only possessions I had to furnish it was a single bed that I had recently acquired from Public`s Own Market, an old rocker recliner and the dishes from my travel trailer. It was like moving into a palace compared to living in the little trailer. Happy with the new surroundings and the amount of space, I realized I could do as much painting as I wanted to do.

Later that fall Dawn and I were looking at each other and wondering what should be next in our lives. Could I live with Dawn`s two teen-age children?
Could they live with and accept me with their mother?
Could I be a step-father to them, and would they be happy about our situation? Would I be distracting their mother`s attention from them? How would Dawn handle discipline with them? Would we really blend together as a family? I pondered and pondered, and I think that Dawn was doing the same.

We were together often, and sometimes I would bring Dawn over to the apartment, or we would go out for an evening lunch. Often we would go to the Moose Lodge, as they had a small bar on the premises and we would have a glass of brandy. There was a juke-box in the place, and sometimes we would dance to a slow waltz; the emotions were starting to run high, and we wanted to be together more and more.

Dawn and I had been spending a lot of time with each other for more than six months. We had been open and honest with each other on all aspects of discussion. We had both experienced previous marriages. Dawn was recently divorced, and I was in the process of divorce. It was mid-life for both of us, as our thoughts went back and forth with recollections of our lives about where we had come from, and where we were headed. Dawn had spoken with her children and they understood her feelings. Within a few more weeks our lives including her children, seemed to quietly fall into place. We set-up home all together, and that`s when our life really started to move forward.

By mid November, we had settled in our apartment and Dawn returned to working in a secretarial pool. The experience of the Artisan` Gallery was behind us, and we had lost nothing when we moved out. The building was under lock and key, apparently permanently closed, and all artisans had left.

Working in a secretarial pool meant Dawn was called to work as a temporary replacement in local offices. She was a qualified legal secretary and there was always work for her when she wanted it. She liked her job. She liked being able to pick and choose and say when she was available.

Dawn`s mother lived in Victoria on Vancouver Island. Dawn frequently phoned, so her mother knew much about me and now our living together. She wanted to come up for a visit, she said, and "check me out." Gertie would arrive in three days on a Friday evening.

Dawn cautioned me about having too much booze around.
She said Gertie, as she preferred to be called, could be
unpredictable with her words if she had been holding
hands with Johnny Walker, or with Calona Royal Red.

I had a "mickey" of rye in the kitchen cupboard, and was
at the kitchen table sipping on rye and water when a
knock sounded at the door. In came Gertie, a bit ahead of
her expected arrival time. She was a tiny women with
grey hair, almond-shaped sparkling brown eyes, and with
a devilish smile from ear to ear.

*"You must be Bob!"* She exclaimed.
*"Yes...would you join me for a small drink?"* I asked.
*"Let`s have it!"* She responded.
I poured an ounce in a water glass and moved the water
pitcher over so she could help herself. She didn`t touch
the water jug, but downed the rye in one shot then shoved
her glass back across the table to the little bottle. It wasn`t
a full bottle, so I poured her another little shot and topped
up my own glass a bit. This time she sipped a little slower,
as she looked straight at me with a wondering expression.

Dawn was down in the laundry room so Gertie and I
were alone to sit and chatter. I told her how pleased I
was when I learned it was she who changed Archie Grey
Owl from trapping to Conservation. She smiled proudly,
and her face softened with gratification about my knowing
some of her background.

I mentioned to her how I had been raised as a youth in the rural bush of the Thunder Bay, Port Arthur area, and how I had trapped weasels when I was a kid and hunted deer for needed meat. I told her how I remembered the depression years when money was not too plentiful, but that we only took from the Wilderness what we needed. She nodded and smiled at me in acknowledgement. *"It's too bad that more people don't feel the same way about our country."* She said. And when her bright sparkling brown eyes looked straight into mine again, and she showed an understanding smile, I knew that I had acquired another friend.

I got to know Gertie quite well over the next years, and I can't recall ever hearing a harsh word of seriousness between us. I learned that if she didn't like a person they would know about it quickly.

Gertie stayed in Kamloops for a few days but slept over at the home of Dawn's half-sister Katherine. Gertie had married again after Archie died, to Count Eric Moltke, and had Katherine. Katherine was ten years younger than Dawn. We visited back and forth until after a few days Gertie returned to Victoria.

Dawn was happy about my meeting with her mother. She was pleased that the introduction had been pleasant. She felt comfortable now that we had met, and she relaxed within the state of our being together.It was meant to be, she felt, as we seemed to move forward with the building of our life for the future.

In January 1974, my wishes were that we could travel to Spain. Dawn and I talked about it often, and desires increased with both of us. We soon agreed we would go together leaving Vancouver in late March. We planned to take a full month.

Dawn asked her Mom if she would come up while we were away and stay in our apartment with Sandra and Glaze. I talked with my work mate at CN again, and I needed to confirm my time off. Once Gertie agreed and when my leave was arranged, we started planning.

We decided we would fly to London, then travel British Airways from London to Madrid, Spain. We would spend a few days in Madrid, then carry on to Malaga on the Coast of De Sol in the Southern region of the Mediterranean.

One issue requiring careful planning was Dawn's health. She was a diabetic, and had been so since she was nine years old. After learning Dawn would be safe travelling in Spain we applied for our passports. By mid March, we were finally prepared for our exciting journey.

Chapter 2

Our flight left Vancouver around supper time. During the nine-hour flight we got to see the sun setting behind us, then rising again in front of us. As we were arriving Heathrow Airport in London the following morning, we looked out over the roof-tops when on our final approach, and Dawn commented on seeing the rows of little brick dwellings. *"I think we're arriving on set for Coronation Street"*, she remarked. Then we felt the slight bump as the wheels of the big jet touched the runway. It had been a pleasant flight for both of us and I could see Dawn relax as we taxied up to the Terminal.

We didn't have to wait very long before we found our baggage on the turntable. We caught the double-decker bus and headed for Victoria Station. Then we pulled out our travel guide: "How to see Europe on $5.00 a day." We found a Bed and Breakfast for seven pound per night for the two of us, and felt the price was reasonable.

We suddenly felt a need to rest for a while as the jet-lag began to let us know we were both tired. By the time we settled in our accommodation we felt as though we had climbed a mountain. After enjoying the traditional English breakfast of bacon, eggs and toast, we laid down to rest.

Neither of us had been to England before, and this city of ten million people, with most of them rushing in a hustle and bustle manner made us appreciate the smaller settlement of the city of Kamloops, back home. We were really not big-city folks, and now we realized it all the more. Everyone seemed to us to be going down the wrong side of the road, and in a mad rush in doing so.

After resting, we caught the typical black English Austin taxi and headed for Trafalgar Square. The pigeons, the statue of Queen Victoria and the Embassy buildings, made both of us realize we were in a city of ancient history, compared to our home place back in Canada.

We walked around for a while and took a few photos as most tourists do. We soon tired again and decided to go back to our Bed and Breakfast place, and leave our visiting of new places until the next day. We found an English fish and chip shop close to where we were staying, and enjoyed the lunch as we picked the fries and fish from the customary horn-shaped paper container that it was wrapped in.

The next morning after we had breakfast, we got another black taxi cab and went to Madam Tusaud's Wax Museum. We were impressed with the statues of many of the Royal families, Piccaso and many, many others. Then we went to see Buckingham Palace, where Dawn's father had entertained King George V1, Queen Mary and Princess Elizabeth and Princess Margaret in the late 1930's. I took a photo of Dawn standing in front of the gates of the Palace. She felt proud of her father's accomplishments of his work in Conservation, which had taken him from Hastings, England where he had been raised as a little boy, to the stage of Buckingham Palace. She was proud too, of his four books which became classics and still in print. The work of her parents would never be forgotten; they are an important part of British and Canadian history and conservation

Dawn told me more about her father, and how he travelled throughout the United Kingdom giving two lectures each day at a different location. I believe she felt him mingling and speaking amongst the pushing crowds of people. Thousands clamoured to get sight of him and to get close to him, as he spoke about our Great Wilderness and the need to take care of it for generations to come. She was proud of the fame he had achieved. She also realized how much it had exhausted him.
The fame, the travel, the lectures, the writing, the speaking, the total demand on his being, broke his health and he died April 13, 1938 at age 49.

The following day our English visit drew to an end and we boarded British Airways for our flight to Madrid. We arrived in Madrid in late afternoon and settled in to our lodging in a down-town hotel.

It was an older hotel, but clean. We rested for a short time then went out to see some of the down-town area of the city. As we strolled around several city blocks we became aware a number of streets running in various directions off the main thoroughfare, forming a hexagon pattern.

After a short time we found a small bar and had a glass of wine and some food. We found their red wine dry and pleasantly appetising. On this day we had been wearing our light jackets of Navy blue with our Canada Maple Leaf on the lapel. There were several people in the small cafe and some of them were eager to talk to us. They wanted to know about America. We found it somewhat unusual that they linked us with the USA. They didn`t differentiate between Canada and the United States until after we had told them.

We were both sure these people realized that Canada and the United States were separate countries. It was merely their habit of referring to many tourists like ourselves as being Americans. They understood as we spoke, and politely apologised for their habit. They were all a warm and friendly lot.

One young couple had their black lab dog in the cafe with them. This was a sort of eye-opener for us being new to the country. We later found that it was common in many cafe`s for the Spanish people to bring their pets. All that we witnessed were well taken care of and trained to just lay under the table while their owners had lunch or a glass of wine. We particularly noticed the relaxed atmosphere of Spain, and we never saw an inebriated person amongst the lot. Our welcome on this day to Spain was warm, and we both enjoyed our reception.

After socializing with these people in the small cafe and sipping on two or three glasses of wine while we ate, we decided to start back to our hotel. We soon discovered we were totally lost in the maze of streets in Madrid,

running in angles to all directions. We couldn`t find our
hotel.

After wandering around for some time we met with
a policeman and asked for guidance. He spoke very little
English, but when I took the hotel receipt out of my wallet
and showed it to him, he realized we were lost. He
cheerfully directed us to where we had to go.

When we were finally home for the evening we
discovered the toilet wouldn`t flush. I went downstairs,
expecting that once I let the desk clerk know we had a
problem it would be rectified. I then found that the desk
clerk didn`t speak much English. Perhaps because
he could smell the dinner wine I had consumed, he began
to stare at me strangely. Then he demanded my passport.
Being naive, and not too familiar with European travel, I
pulled it out of my jacket pocket to show it to him. He
took it from my hand and after studying it for at least five
minutes, he slipped it into a drawer behind the counter.

I wondered why, because it didn`t seem to me to be a
usual step to get a toilet fixed. When we had first checked
in, and I had been carrying my telescopic painting easel
wrapped in an old painting smock, we may have appeared
threatening.

I again tried to explain what I wanted done. Finally a man
clad in cover-alls came into the front desk area, and
beckoned me with his finger. I didn`t know for sure

what was taking place, but when he beckoned again I followed him back to our room. He was going to solve our problem, but I still didn`t have my passport.

Tired, we tried to rest for the night, but I was nervous about my passport. I couldn`t understand why the man at the front desk felt he wanted to retain it. We were not terrorists, and had done nothing wrong that we realized. The following morning, after tossing and turning for sometime during the night, I went down to the front desk and the man behind the counter handed me my passport; no questions asked. I felt free again.

Following breakfast we went for a walk to see some more of the city. With the old structured stone buildings, we again realized the much longer span of history and civilization than we had at home in Canada. We spotted a man with a horse and carriage parked at the curb of a main street. He was offering sight-seeing tours of down-town Madrid.

The Clydesdale horse was beautifully groomed, and the black leather harness was decorated with brass grommets, and red tassels were attached to the tips of the hames. The carriage was polished black and had a posh red-leather back seat, which could accommodate three people. After speaking with the middle-aged gentleman who apparently owned the horse and carriage, we discovered that for approximately $9.00 our money, he would give us a one-hour tour of down-town Madrid.

We climbed into the carriage and after a couple of customary mouth sounds from the driver, the animal trotted along the main street. We soon took one of the narrow side streets and, of course, had no idea where we were going. By this time of morning. the streets were becoming busy with traffic. Horns tooted, and some people dashed from one side of the street to the other in front of us. Then an auto moving quickly along the thoroughfare, drove onto the sidewalk after a beep on the horn, and the man driving waved at us gleefully and went happily along his way. It was the first horse and carriage ride that Dawn and I ever had in our life. We both chuckled as we realized we had come all the way across the Atlantic to Spain for such an interesting experience. It was a warm and sunny day and we both felt good as I said: *"This is probably the closest we will get to riding a donkey."* Dawn chuckled with an affectionate hold on my hand.

We would leave the next day for our flight to Malaga, on the Mediterranean coast. Dawn usually carried her insulin and medical gadgets in a day bag so to always have them with her. But when we left Madrid on our flight to Malaga, she decided that since it was just a short flight, she would check her day bag along with our baggage.

When we got to the airport, she placed it with our other baggage along with my aluminium extension easel, wrapped in my painting smock, for the staff to check. My easel generated strange looks again and I was beginning to wonder if airport personnel suspected me of carrying a concealed weapon. There was apparently some unrest in the Basque Region of Northern Spain, but we were not aware of any serious problems. Perhaps that was the reason for the curious manners of staff as we passed through to the departure area.

We boarded the Spanish aircraft, and after a couple of hours we landed in Malaga. When we tried to find our baggage we discovered there was no baggage for us to be found. What has happened, we wondered? How could it have disappeared on such a short flight?

Then we remembered Dawn's insulin was in the baggage. Suddenly we were in a very serious predicament. We waited at the Malaga airport for another hour nervously hoping our baggage would show up. No such luck! It was strange, and now with being nervous it had become an intriguing situation very difficult to understand. We began to wonder what would happen next to us in this far-off foreign country.

Dawn would need her insulin later that evening. I could see the frowns of anxiety and concern on her face. We waited for another hour in hope the baggage would appear, before giving our beach-front hotel phone number to airport officials so they could contact us.

We caught a taxi to the hotel and checked in. When we got up to our fifth-floor accommodation and opened the door, we found it was a beautiful suite. It overlooked

the Mediterranean and the sandy beaches along front of
the hotel row. Then when we checked the fridge, we
found it stocked with various small sample bottles of
liquor and wine.

We started to discuss what we could do about Dawn's
insulin and our missing luggage. Because of her diabetes,
we couldn't just wait the problem out before she would
need her insulin injection. I phoned the airport to see if
our baggage had been located. It had not! Dawn and I
decided that we should try and contact a local Spanish
doctor, and explain to him our problem and Dawn's lack
of insulin. We were a fortunate couple. The doctor agreed
to come over to the hotel and meet with us. He gave
Dawn a prescription but by then it was too late that day to
get insulin from a pharmacy.

The Spanish doctor didn't charge us for the call. We
offered him whatever such a call would normally cost. He
merely smiled and said *"We like to take care of our
visitors, and we like them to come back again. Next time,
don't lose your insulin!"* He smiled as he got up to leave
and we thanked him deeply for calling upon us.

Early the next morning the phone rang in our unit, and an
airport official announced that our baggage had been
located. We went to the airport and picked it up, but
nobody could tell us where it had been.

We were soon settled in our feelings, then after breakfast
we went out for a walk. The area where we had our
apartment was along the high tourist area of the coast.

We headed towards the city centre to see some of the old part of the city, along with the major business district.

By this time we needed to cash more of our travellers cheques for exchange to the Spanish Passeta. When we went into a major bank, we particularly noticed that the staff were all young men, and all neatly dressed in dark suits and tie. Not a lady was in sight in the bank office. It seemed to us that the men were the bread winners of the families, and the ladies stayed home to take care of the house and children. We thought it very unusual for a bank staff.

Dawn and I accepted most cities as being very similar, and felt it was of more interest to see how different the people were. Dawn looked in a couple of ladies' dresswear stores, and commented that the staff were mostly young ladies. When we went into a few of the restaurants, we noticed the waiters were usually young boys.

Then we reached the waterfront and docks of the old part of the city. There were fish shops nearby selling fresh fish, and there were some men selling fish from a dockside table where their boats were tied up. When I saw this area it reminded me of my home town of Port Arthur, and the fish docks on the North shore of Lake Superior. When I was a youth in the 1940's, and when the herring season was on, the fish were spread out on the wooden docks so they would freeze during the nights. Then they were packed in boxes in ice for distribution.

We entered a small cafe to have some lunch. There were plenty of fish dishes and chicken to choose from, but beef was seldom an available choice. We both felt welcome in the small outlets from the smiles and warm greetings we experienced. When we finally had some lunch, I chose smoked fish, a small diner roll and a bottle of Cerveza, (beer). Dawn had a glass of wine and chicken. Again we noticed that frequently people would have their dogs with them; well trained, as they lay under the tables in waiting for their masters to finish lunch.

We learned there would be a large Easter Float parade that evening along the main streets of Malaga. We understood that most of the people were of the Catholic Faith. We wanted to witness this parade and decided to come back to the city centre that evening. It was only six or eight blocks from our accommodation.

When we came back into town early that evening, the streets were packed with people. All were walking slowly along to the central area where the parade would start. We noticed too, that with thousands of people moving slowly along the sidewalks, there was no pushing or shoving. The people seemed very well mannered and gentle as they moved along. We were fascinated with the crowd behaviour.

After following people we finally came to the place where the huge religious floats were preparing themselves to start the parade. One large float was mounted on long bars, and it must have been 25 or

30 feet in length. It had a high open canopy with Mary
and the Christ child seated within. Then there were
hundreds of candles, all lighted.

We watched closely to see how this float would move
along the street. It was huge. Then, at least twenty men,
along each bar along each side, and all dressed in black
tuxedo suits and bow ties, stood close, almost to touch
each other, and all facing forward waiting for a command.
The one gentleman who was leading that particular float,
then gave a command to lift. Upward the float raised until
the bars down each side rested on the rows of shoulders.
A forward command was given and
the carriers, in unison step, moved forward, and the big
float moved gently along in unison with all the other floats
in the parade.

It was a spectacular sight to see the huge float shouldered
by black-suited men, with the high mounted Christ child
and the burning candles, all which moved along with a
slight swaying motion. A very dramatic display showing
their dedication to the Christian Faith.

The next evening we went into a small night-club cafe to
listen to a couple of Spanish guitarists play their melodies,
along with a young black-haired, slim lady
singing Spanish tunes. As we sat and sipped slowly on a
Sangria cocktail, we enjoyed the song and music of *"Blue
Spanish Eyes."* Then the Spanish group took a break and
a group of American tourists, somewhat inebriated,
without music, made asses of themselves by

boisterously singing, "The Beer Barrel Polka." What a
farce and let-down! We finished our drink and left
for our hotel, realizing that in the touristy areas, the
behaviour of a few people on holidays have very little
ambience to add to the respect for the Spanish artistry.

On another night we fully enjoyed a larger night-club with
Flamenco Dancing. We felt the complete atmosphere
vibrating when a long line of Flamenco dancers
entertained. They were colourful, proud,
and beautiful to watch. That evening was most pleasant.

A few days later we decided to rent a car and drive
through some of small interior towns. Driving was easy
for us there, as different from England, they drove on the
right-hand side of the road as we do at home. After
driving some thirty or so miles in from the Mediterranean
coast, we came to a small town called Alora. We parked
our rented car and strolled some of the streets, looking in
some of the small shops and having coffee in one of the
cafes. After walking and looking around town some
more, we realized it was getting close to our supper time.

In this village, all the houses were typically white and
perched in rows along the gentle slopes of the hillside.
We liked the atmosphere of the town and decided we
would overnight there. In talking casually with a few
people in the shops, we met an elderly gentleman who
apparently had been a world traveller. He told us he had
visited the Swiss Alps and had seen the Canadian
Rockies, and now he was retired.

When we asked him about a nice place to stay overnight, he immediately wanted to direct us to a favourable place. He walked us part way up the gentle hillside on a side street, and introduced us to the people who owned and operated a neat little dining spot and who apparently rented overnight accommodation. After he introduced us to the lady inside, he left and we thanked him for being so gracious in meeting, and for showing us where we could spend the night.

The home, I recall, was not large, but the dining room had a huge oak table and matching chairs that could seat ten people. It appeared as though they did special catering by reservation only. The lady asked if we would come back in about two hours to have our supper.

Following some driving around the town and nearby area, we came back and were shown what would be our room for the night. It was a small room, beautifully kept, and in the corner was a tiny cabinet with a porcelain wash basin and porcelain water pitcher. It was a decorative feature, as the regular bathroom was down a narrow hallway.

It struck me as being Victorian and Dawn loved the quietness of the place. It also carried my memories back to one of the first small CN stations I had worked at in Ontario during the 1940`s. At that time I had stayed in a small country hotel, and in my room was a little stand with a porcelain wash basin and water pitcher for daily use.

"Dinner was ready",said the Spanish hostess as she guided us to the big oak table in the dining room. She brought us a litre of red wine along with two crystal wine glasses, then proceeded to pour just enough in each glass for a customary taste. " Is it ok?" She asked.
When we spoke our approval she placed the bottle on the table in front of us, then left to bring our dinner. The meal we had was a delicious roast chicken, based in rich, pure orange juice and with an orange wedge placed on the edge of each plate.

We thoroughly enjoyed this atmosphere as we feasted on the dinner and sipped the red wine. We both felt we were getting a Royal welcome. We took much time with our diner and wine, then went to our small comfortable room and slept soundly all night.

The next morning we left town with our little Spanish car, feeling so grateful for the man who took us to the lodging the previous day. We drove  further into the interior, expecting we would meet some more very nice people, and we certainly did. We were away from the bustling noise of the tourist coast, and the sometimes false sophistication of those  who thrive  in high density tourist spots. We were in our elements of a slower pace of life, and the generosity and warm personal welcome with people we met, in these off-the-main-drag little villages.

The next village we arrived at was smaller, but the houses again were all white and perched along the hillside. This town had only one main street, and we could have driven through the village in less than two minutes. We stopped on the one and only main road and went into a small cafe to have lunch.

Dawn visited with the man and lady owners and they became intrigued as she spoke about our home back in Canada. She told them about her father and mother and their living with two beavers in the wilderness. They were fascinated with her talking and showing them the photo of her father bottle feeding a baby beaver. Then they offered us accommodation for a few days with meals at a very reasonable rate of $9.00 per day. That`s what we calculated with the exchange of our money to Spanish Passetas.

We decided to stay with these people for three or four days, as we were pleased with their offer of hospitality. This was another opportunity to learn about local people, we thought. Our room was much the same as our accommodation of the previous night. The bathroom was straight across the hall from our room.An archway at the back of the house led us to a small courtyard with flower beds, stone walkways and marble bird baths and feeders.

In the main house, the marble floors with scatter rugs warmed the atmosphere. Our landlords obviously spoke with their neighbours, telling them about Grey Owl and about the beaver, and how we were visiting from Canada. Later that afternoon, an elderly couple arrived to visit and meet with us.

After Dawn spoke with them and showed them some photos, they invited us for lunch the next day. We accepted the invitation with pleasure, and we went to their home very neatly kept and landscaped with a small lawn and beds of beautiful roses and other colourful flowers. We sat around their dining room table as they poured wine and showed us family photos. We could easily understand them, as they spoke English quite well. They were a warm couple, proud and dignified. We lunched on tasty soup and warm slices of home made bread. It was delightful and comforting to be welcomed in such a manner.

After lunch they asked us to walk with them to the town centre, where we could get fresh fruit and vegetables from a farm truck parked there. It allowed people to make fresh purchases, and quite a number of ladies were gathered by the truck when we arrived. After buying and paying for their produce, they held up their apron by the bottom hem. This formed a bowl-shape, where the vendor placed their fruit and veggies. They seemed to be a very happy lot as they headed off home with their aprons full.

We asked our hosts if we could purchase fruit for them, as a token of our appreciation for their hospitality. They thanked us, but declined.They invited us to tour the town area with them and we accepted. We enjoyed seeing some of the sights and meeting some of their friends.

As we sauntered along, a chubby little man dressed in a military uniform and with a big rifle slung over his shoulder, and riding a motorcycle, suddenly drove out from a narrow side lane. He waved, a big smile on his face, then rode off down the street. The next morning we enjoyed having breakfast outside, where the hosts` big red Labrador dog joined us, lying on the table at the far end. That day we strolled the village by ourselves. We walked by a huge estate near the outskirts of the little town, and noticed the entrance to the property was blocked by a huge black iron gate. Then we turned around, and when we were half-way back to town, the little fellow with the big gun sped past us on his motorcycle heading towards the mansion. Three or four minutes later, zoom, he passed us heading into town again, smiling and waving. We continued on our stroll, and as we reached the little school, we stopped and watched young boys playing a game of soccer.

We then returned to our lodging. This style of being tourists suited us, and added to another lovely day. We wanted to thank our hosts in some special way for their hospitality. I dug my paints and easel out from our baggage and began painting a small landscape of the area, while Dawn sorted through her photographs of her father with the beavers. The day we left we gave them the little landscape and a photo, and enjoyed how our gifts pleased them. At least a dozen people showed up to bid us a happy journey, and to come back again, if we ever returned to Spain.

We had thoroughly enjoyed our stay in the village, and the warm and welcoming people. Our hosts gave us a bottle of Anisette as we departed. Through the rear-view mirror I could see many friendly hands waving. Dawn and I smiled at each other. Spain was special.

Our next Spanish adventure was to Algeciras, a coastal town on the Straight of Gibraltar. We could see the huge rock just a few miles out in the sea. We obtained accommodation in a small hotel. Within a few hours we sensed some tension in the area. Apparently relations between Spain and Britain were becoming increasingly strained.

Along the waterfront docks we could see a lot of military men "armed with guns." We didn't know what the problem was, but we realized that we best not go around wandering and asking a lot of questions.

We ate in a small cafe, and walked some of the streets as though everything was normal. We stayed to ourselves without anyone bothering us. The next day we caught the ferry which crossed the Straight to the Spanish port of Ceuta, Morocco. We disembarked the ferry at the area of the industrial part of the city. As we walked the street leading away from the Port industrial buildings towards the main business area of the city, several men approached us offering to exchange our Spanish money, to the Moroccan Durham. We knew to wait until we reached a Government outlet. Three young boys persistently grabbed at our elbows wanting to be our guides for the day. At first we told them that as we would not be travelling very far, we were stopping at a restaurant before deciding anything. We would think about it after we had something to eat. One of the young boys continued following us from the Port area to the town; it seemed we had a guide whether we hired him or not. When we came across a government exchange we traded some Spanish money for the Moroccan Durham.

As we continued to walk into the city centre, we saw many military men on the streets. We sauntered along trying to avoid drawing any unusual attention to ourselves. Two boys with goats on a leash came dashing out from a lane. We paused momentarily as they rushed by us on their way.

We purposely had not worn our jackets with the Maple Leaf, so as to not be too conspicuous. We had been told before we came, that it was unwise to dress like well-off tourist travellers. So far we had not been bothered by anyone, other than the boys wanting to guide us.
We finally arrived at a bus depot where we could get some food. Our mint tea and small portion of chicken, and slice of bread tasted good, and filled us.

After relaxing, we decided to travel on to Tetouan. Soon we were on a bus loaded with Arabs of all ages heading south along a dusty road. Two women, seated a few rows behind us were obviously having an argument, and were gradually becoming louder with each other in their own language. After travelling a short way, the driver suddenly stopped the bus, and the vehicle was quickly boarded by several soldiers all carrying rifles. They were obviously looking for a particular person, as moments after we stopped, they escorted one man off the bus.

We carried on, never to know what that incident was all about.

When we arrived in the centre of Tetouan, we discovered our one young persistent guide had travelled with us to the city on the same bus. Now we wanted him to guide us through the bustling streets, and show us the Casba area. Before long, we walked down a narrow street that led to the Casba market area.

It was a sudden change of pace to what we had experienced on the streets of mainland Spain. The streets were crowded with numerous small shops and sidewalk vendors. People were loud and pushing to what they wanted. It was an aggressive area of the city, we felt. Dawn and I noticed a little elderly lady sitting on a blanket on the ground. It appeared she was selling four apples, carefully arranged in the centre of her blanket. She was staring into space and seemed dazed.

We continued to walk along, until we arrived at a building housing youthful carvers. We went inside where they were creating beautiful hand-crafted jewellery boxes. Some of the young boys approached us begging for money, but our guide warned us not to give them any. If they were found to be begging they would be in serious trouble with the management.

After touring Tetouan's many shops, and where I had purchased a wide-brimmed leather fedora, we decided not to stay overnight. By the time we boarded a bus heading back to Ceuta, and the ferry port docks, it was

late evening and dark. Dawn and I and one Arab
gentleman were the only people on that return bus
journey.

We had travelled only a short distance when we came to
a sudden stop, and the driver got out. It appeared to us as
though we were in the middle of nowhere, then we saw
the driver head for a dimly lit window of a house along
side of the road. Leaving us on the bus we had no idea
what was taking place, but we were becoming
increasingly nervous. We asked the Arab gentleman, our
polite fellow passenger, where along the bus route we
might find accommodation to safely stay overnight. We
decided we could return to mainland Spain the next day in
daylight.He informed us of a tavern another few miles up
the road that had rooms for rent. About thirty minutes
later, the bus driver returned and we were finally on the
move again.

When he pulled into the parking area of the dimly-lit
tavern, we got out of the bus and went inside.We spoke to
the bartender who assured us we would be welcome to
a room for the night. I ordered a glass of beer and Dawn
had a small glass of wine. There were only two couples in
the bar. The bar tender offered us a small fish on a plate,
heavily salted and smoked. We had much difficulty eating
it but struggled with it as it was only a small fish.

Following our little snack and drink, we were led up a
very narrow stairway to our room. The whole atmosphere
seemed mysterious and a bit scary to us. We were

already in this situation and could do nothing to change it. The next morning after a restless night in what turned out to be a lumpy bed, we caught another bus to the ferry docks. We were happy to be going back across the Straight of Gibralter, to mainland Spain.

We decided to travel up the Spanish coast as far as Estapona, as the Malaga area was too touristy, we felt. When we got to the bus depot we purchased our tickets, and soon arrived in Estapona. When we got off the bus we bought some bread, cheese and a bottle of wine. Then Dawn and I walked across the main highway away from the beach area to look for accommodation. We were lucky again. We got a comfortable room, although it was not beach front, which overlooked the Mediterranean, for $4.50 per night. We decided to spend a few days here before returning to the City of Malaga.

In our wandering, we found a Spanish night club and discovered from the poster on the door there was a concert of Spanish guitarists and dancers that evening. We decided to go and make it our evening entertainment. There was an audience of about fifty people, and we once again enjoyed the evening .

A few days later we boarded a bus for Malaga where we would spend overnight before heading to the airport, and the last leg of our journey home. When we arrived for our International flight we learned that Air Canada was in the middle of a pilot's strike. We were told that flights were still being flown from London to Montreal, so we flew from Malaga to Madrid then on to Heathrow in London.

It was chaotic at the Air Canada counter at Heathrow, as staff tried to accommodate the many travellers wanting to get back to Canada. We learned we could get a flight from London to Montreal, but continuing on to Vancouver may pose a problem. Upon our arrival in Montreal, there was along line of customers, all waiting for something to happen. When we approached the Air Canada counter we were told that we did not have a flight to Vancouver.

Dawn and I were casually dressed in old jeans and I was wearing the leather fedora I had purchased in the Casba of Morocco. I was also carrying my telescopic easel wrapped in my painting smock. We must have looked like the Beverly Hillbillies, but I explained to Air Canada Customer Service a second time, and they finally offered us overnight hotel accommodation in Montreal. They supplied us with a taxi to get there. When we strolled up to the reception counter of the posh hotel, at least half a dozen people in the lobby stared straight through us, apparently wondering what kind of clientele we were, and from where. We checked in and slept well.

The next morning after a courtesy breakfast in the dining room, we queried Air Canada staff at the airport as to what flight would we be on to get back to Vancouver. Chaos again! We were asked to remain at the hotel at Air Canada`s expense and to contact them later in the day.

So there we were in Montreal, waiting for our flight but we were not free to gallivant or sight-see as it was a standby situation. However, the staff at the hotel took good care of us.

Early that evening the airline staff informed us that we could get a morning flight from Montreal to Vancouver. It was too late to think about going out of the hotel and to any downtown area, so we went into the hotel lounge for a quiet drink, watched tv on the big screen they had, and quietly passed the evening.

Finally, three days after we left London we were back home in our Kamloops apartment telling Gertie about our experiences in both Spain and Morocco. I was actually content that we made the journey that I had dreamt of, and that I had made it with Dawn. We were happy together, just me and, "Little Big Mouth" .

At home in Kamloops, Dawn returned to the secretarial pool and I was back at my duties as Rail Traffic Controller with CN. We had enjoyed our Spanish and Moroccan travels and liked telling about them to our friends and acquaintances. Gertie went home to Victoria, and Dawn and I and her two children were once again together in our apartment.

Chapter 3

Back to our routine, after taking a little time to get the settled-in feeling again as the result of travels, we visited Margie at the clothing store. We took periodic drives into the country, and the occasional trip to Savona. Since I was a Past Governor of The Loyal Order of Moose, we attended the Saturday night socials and danced late into the night.

We had now been together for almost a year, and in doing so we gained many new friends. We also liked travelling together so much that in the fall of 1974, we were planning a journey to Ontario for the summer of 1975. I believed we would now need a new vehicle for travelling comfort, and purchased a 1975 Dodge Van. With Dawn`s help and ideas we planned on making it into a camper and customized just for us. It would be nice for our leisurely travels. We started planning our travel plans that would suit the two of us.

Coming originally from Ontario I had relatives in the Thunder Bay area. I naturally wanted them to meet Dawn. We also wanted to visit Beaver Lodge, Grey Owl`s cabin in the Prince Albert National Park. Having seen Dawn`s many photographs I was excited in seeing her father`s cabin, as well as looking forward to the extended trip we were planning. Our shared life together continued to be interesting for both of us.

I had worked for CN in Prince Albert in the 1950`s. I had friends there as well. So we were both going back to familiar places and people. We laughed  when we realized that we had both been living in Prince Albert at the same time.

We celebrated New Years of 1975. Then to lessen my usual mid-winter blues we began to plan exactly what we would do to make our new van into a comfortable camper. I purchased styrofoam for seat cushions, and would make benches and a drop-leaf table across the back of the van to make into a bed. Dawn picked up some fabric on sale for cushions, and within a short time she made covers to custom fit.

We purchased from a friend of mine, a counter with a built-in sink and icebox, and I installed it lengthwise behind the driver's seat. With our combined efforts, by time April warm weather arrived we had our travel accommodation all decked out. We looked forward to its comfort and pleasurable travels.

As well as working on our van during the winter, I had painted a number of landscapes. The public library in Valleyview, located in the South end of town, let me use their display room to exhibit my work. At the request of the library the local press took photos of a few of my paintings and wrote a supportive column. The following week my show drew over a hundred visitors. I was pleased with the event. Some paintings sold, and I was asked to do a couple of commissions.

Dawn was also experiencing community support. She was dedicated to the environmental movement across the country, which was growing stronger, and was asked to

speak to children in a local elementary school. She was happy for any opportunity to teach children, like her father before her. She felt that talking with children helped them learn to take special interest in wildlife, and to value our wilderness in the Great Canadian forests.
She shared the thoughts of her parents Grey Owl and Anahareo, and would often say: *"We must learn to live together with respect, and take only what we need."* The children listened attentively.

In late June, 1975, we began our journey eastward to Thunder Bay, departing Kamloops by the Yellowhead, travelling towards Jasper. We had a full month for our journey, which meant we could drive at our leisure, needing to achieve only two or three hundred miles each day.

Our first stop was at the Mount Robson Provincial Park. After setting up camp, the fire crackled and burned well, as the campground's wood was dry. We brought out the bottle of brandy from where it had been carefully stored in our camper, chipped some ice from our own ice box, sat by the fire, chatting and sipping on brandy and water. We even had proper brandy glasses for celebrating our first trip in the new camper van. We were travelling again together. Dawn and I never ran short of conversation, and we savoured being together. Compatible travellers, we were! Brandy, bonfires, and
long evening conversations were daily highlights for both of us.

Three days later we arrived at the Municipal Campground on the outskirts of Prince Albert. Our first stop was a visit with Mrs. Winters, now a widow part of the family who raised Dawn for many of her childhood years after her father's death, in April of 1938. We also visited with one of my older train dispatcher friends whom I had worked with in the 1950's. He was now retired. Being in Prince Albert was like old home week for both of us.

Following two days in the Prince Albert campground we headed north to Waskesiu, located in the Prince Albert National Park. Here we were to meet with Parks Canada Chief Naturalist, Merv Syroteuk, who would take us across Lake Kingsmere to the north end of the lake. From there it would be a two-mile hike to the cabin, where Dawn, as a youngster, had romped and played with Jelly Roll, the beaver. It was also where her father was at rest. Both of us felt excited about starting the long-anticipated journey, as it took a full day to make the return trip from Waskesiu.

I had fished on Lake Kingsmere in the 1950's while working at Prince Albert. So I had a good idea about the crossing of it from one end to the other, and how treacherous it could get at times, especially in the afternoons if the wind should suddenly get up. We were not worried, as Parks staff would take us across in a large power boat. I often wondered how Grey Owl and Anahareo crossed by canoe, in an upcoming storm. Perhaps they took shelter at times.

Dawn was looking forward to sharing the experience with me, as her father's cabin had been designated as a National Historic site by Parks Canada. She was anxious to see it again as well as her father's grave. It had been a few years since she had been there.

The morning we arrived at Waskesiu, we met with Merv at the Parks office. Then we travelled by truck to the south end of Lake Kingsmere. We loaded a small back-pack containing our lunch into the power boat and within ten minutes we were cutting through the waves of Kingsmere on our way to the north end.

When we arrived at the landing, we discovered that a group of young girl-guides were camping there. Then we noticed a young black bear up on his hind legs, scratching at the outdoor toilet, trying desperately to climb to the roof-top. We assumed that the large pack-sack resting upon the roof of the outhouse must have contained some camping food. The young black bear who obviously had scented the food, was determined to get at it. Merv told us that this bear had made a nuisance of itself on other occasions, and now explained that Parks people were to live-trap it for re location. There were no signs of any other bears in the vicinity.

During our hike along the pathway to Grey Owl's cabin, we stopped for a short time at the south end of Lake Ajawaan. This was the half-mile portage from Lake Kingsmere, which Grey Owl and Anahareo had packed many times during their years up there.I could see at this point, Dawn was deep in thought about her parents and how it came about that they were located in this wilderness.

Grey Owl was born as Archie Belaney in Hastings, England in 1888. As a child he fantasized about the American Indians after seeing a touring Buffalo Bill show. Archie dreamt as a kid about someday going to Canada and meeting the Red Skins as he referred to them. Archie's dreams became true, as it was spoken by one of the Indian Chiefs whom we met: *"A man can become what he dreams, and Archie had dreamt well."* He lectured on conservation throughout Eastern Canada, the United States, and throughout the United Kingdom. His major lecture was entertaining the Royal Family in Buckingham Palace in 1937. .

While Anahareo was not the public speaker that Grey Owl was, after his death she continue to support his ideals, and continued for the rest of her life to emphasise the need for conservation of both wild life and our Canadian Wilderness. In 1975, she was Honoured by the International League for The Rights of Animals. She was Honoured by the City of Kamloops in 1979, and in 1983, she was awarded The Order of Canada. All awards were for her work in conservation.

Dawn, the daughter of these world famous parents, after becoming an adult picked up the spark of conservation that her world famous parents had started working on many years before. As we stood quietly on the southern shore of Lake Ajawaan, we both looked across the expanse of water and could see the cabin of Beaver Lodge, nestled tightly to the shoreline at the north end of the lake. It was here, at this cabin, where Dawn had romped and played as a child with the beavers named Jelly Roll and Rawhide. They were her playmates as a little girl during the time she was there.

I saw a single tear trickle down Dawn`s cheek as she was reminiscing some of her childhood life. The back of my neck tingled as I stood silently beside her in this quiet wilderness area. Merv glanced towards us, and I knew immediately he understood the drama of our visit. It was the deepest spiritual experience I had ever felt in my life.

We broke the silence as we started to walk the pathway again, as it wound its way amongst aspen, birch and spruce for another mile and a half to the cabin. Along the way a  slight breeze whispered through the leaves. Dawn and I both felt the sense and touch of solitude, and we believed we were very close and in harmony with the Spirit of the wilderness..

When we arrived on the knoll above the lake, looking down upon the cabin I realized we had reached the epitome of our journey. Here we felt the calm and serene atmosphere as we paused and gazed  out far over the cabin`s roof to the distant shore. Then off to the side of the knoll where we were standing, I saw the large wooden cross over Grey Owl`s grave. I recalled what Dawn had told me when we first met, about her father once having said: "*Between these poplars at my cabin, is where I want to rest.*" I sensed that his wishes became true, and he was at Peace with the world.

The call of a loon broke the silence as we walked down towards the cabin on the lakeshore. I left Dawn's side and looked through the open doorway of the cabin. The lakeside of the small room had no floor. What was there amazed me. The structure of a beaver lodge made up of criss-crossed bone-dry pieces of poplar and alder were neatly arranged. Although It had been abandoned by the beavers and felt lifeless, I could easily visualize Jelly Roll and Rawhide entering through the open door of the cabin during the 1930's, while pushing smaller pieces of poplar across the floor to the proper spot of their own private structure; closely shared by the two people who protected them.

Then I visualized little Dawn just outside the cabin, nose-to-nose with Jelly Roll, as the photo she had shown me. It all came to life within my imagination. As we sat around outside upon the ground, I looked across at Dawn's face. She was deep in thought, back in the happy times of the ebb of her childhood of time gone by, feeling grateful for the uniqueness of all her memories.

We didn't talk much as we opened the small back-pack, munched on sandwhiches and drank fresh juice. After lunch I held Dawn's hand firmly as we started on our return hike, climbed the knoll, took one look back, and departed for Waskesiu.

Dawn and I had been together for more than a year, and after sharing many quiet discussions during that time, we had developed a spiritual compatibility between us.

When I was in my early 30`s, long before I had ever met Dawn, I had searched and searched for a deeper purpose in life. I had read Spinoza and many others, as I tried to satisfy my hunger. In 1974, to celebrate the fullness of Dawn`s and my growing together, and the wilderness journeys we took, I wrote the following lines. Dawn liked the writing.

" *I love to roam beyond where the city ends,*

*To a place where, long ago, I had waiting friends;*

*Across a field and amongst the pines,*

*To a pond and deep ravine;*

*An obscure place which only but a few have ever seen.*

*I stood beside a cedar by a brook,*

*Where once I held a willow, line and hook;*

*I saw a furry friend on a path that I once trod;*

*I felt a gentle breeze; I sensed the touch of God.*"

*******

Following our journey to lake Ajawaan and the visit to Beaver Lodge, we sincerely thanked Merv Syroteuk of Parks Canada for safely guiding us on the trip across Lake Kingsmere, then on to the cabin. We were grateful to Parks Canada for their assistance in having a wonderful day.

On our return to Prince Albert the following day, we camped again in the Municipal Campground. We were staying over, as Dawn had promised Mrs. Winters we would have lunch with her on our return.

Mrs. Winters was always happy to see Dawn, as she was like a daughter to her. I was happy to have had the opportunity of meeting this lady as well. She had cared much for Dawn in raising her for most of the time during Dawn`s childhood.

Following lunch the next day, we drove north to the village of Christopher Lake, where Mrs. Winter`s son, Stan and wife Irene had a cottage. We parked overnight in their yard so Dawn could visit again with Stan. As a young boy, he had spent part of the summer of 1936 with Archie at Beaver Lodge. His older sister, Margaret, a trained stenographer, had typed Grey Owl`s manuscript, " *Tales of an Empty Cabin*," for him, before he`d first sent it to the publisher.

During that evening, Stan and Irene took us to nearby Bell`s Beach, a night spot, where we danced and shared a couple of beers, as Dawn and Stan reminisced about their earlier lives.

After leaving the Prince Albert area, we planned to stop at Wasagaming, in the Riding Mountain National Park.

We arrived at dusk, and as we drove down the main street, Dawn saw a neon sign reading "Grey Owl's Steak and Pizza." I recognized this was a problem, one Dawn would want to do something about. I now understood Dawn's respect for her father and her wish that all reference to him, or use of his name, be respectful to the family..

Her father had been recognized world-wide as a Conservationist. She felt hurt that Grey Owl's reputation as a writer and conservationist could be used in association with steak and pizza. His name was her's to protect. No permission had been given to the owner of this restaurant.

The next morning, we met with the Superintendent of the Park, and Dawn expressed her concerns about the unsuitable sign. The Supt. offered to see what could be done about it. Since Grey Owl's cabin had been created as a National Historic Site in Riding Mountain by Parks Canada, it was his concern, too. We learned later the sign had been removed.

We planned to visit the Grey Owl cabin in Riding Mountain National Park. It was a five-mile hike from the outskirts of Wasagaming, so left early the next morning with back-pack equipped with fresh fruit juice and sandwiches. We needed nourishment, as we would be hiking ten miles there and back. The path was well trod, and was a winter ski trail, so it was easy walking. It would have been a very full day by the time we got back to our van. This lake where Grey Owl's cabin was located was much smaller than Lake Ajawaan.

The lake had a lot of algae around it, and as Archie felt it was not suitable for the beaver, he stayed there for only six months before requesting a move by Parks Canada. The Parks accommodated his request for the move to Lake Ajawaan, after Grey Owl had scouted the new area, and found it was where he wanted to relocate.

As we walked, Dawn told me her father developed some dislike for the local RCMP in Wasagaming during his brief stay there. Perhaps because of difficulties he'd had with the Ontario Provincial Police of his early years in the Biscotasing area in Ontario.

Apparently when Archie happened to be in town in Wasagaming, and went into the restaurant to eat, if a police constable happened to be there at the same time, Archie would choose a booth directly across from the policeman, eye him up and down, then take his hunting knife out and rub his fingers back and forth along the sharp blade while glancing at the cop eye-to-eye. Dawn often chuckled as she told me these stories about her father.

When we actually got to the lake and Dawn saw the cabin, while she appreciated the structure and size of it, the open area around it did not have the dense wilderness feeling. She said it did not have the feeling of seclusion and protection. She seemed to feel her father had made a good decision in asking to be relocated. With a laugh, she said to me, *"I was probably conceived in this cabin!"*

We sat on a bench in front of the cabin and had our lunch. By the time we arrived back at our camper we were both tired and exhausted from the long journey. I made our usual bonfire, then we sipped on a brandy and water before going to bed for the night.

The next morning we had coffee with Marge Ringstrom and her husband. Marge wrote local news articles, and wanted to speak to us about our day`s journey. Dawn told her that her hopes were to visit all the places possible where her parents had lived over the years they were together. She told Marge how she appreciated the warm welcome we experienced with Parks staff when we had first arrived.

Our next stop was Winnipeg after we left Riding Mountain National Park. I had worked for CN there in the late 1940`s, first as a telegraph operator in the Fort Rouge office, then when I was trained in Rail Traffic Control in 1949. Dawn looked forward to meeting some of my old friends, and as we chatted I recalled myself as a young man of 21 at the time. We visited and toured for three days, then left Winnipeg and headed for Port Arthur, Ontario, home of many of my relatives and family.

Dawn was interested in our visits there, and meeting many relatives and other folks whom I had known since

childhood. After a five-day visit and enjoying good times
in Port Arthur, we said goodbye and left. Our travel
itinerary scheduled us to visits in Atikokan, Fort Frances,
Rainy River, and another short stop in Winnipeg. Then
we  headed west and arrived back home in Kamloops,
four weeks to the day from when we had left.

It was back to work again  for me with CN, and Dawn
returned to secretarial work a few days later. By fall, we
were already talking and planning again, options  for the
summer of 1976. We decided we wanted to travel east
again through to Ottawa, then south into the  United
States, and back towards home through the midwestern
states.

That journey took us to Ottawa, then south across the
U.S. border to a small town in New Jersey. We went there
to visit a lady named, Hope Sawyer, who lives in a rural
area close to a beaver pond. She was the organizer of a
group called *"The Beaver Defenders"*, and had
been a dedicated follower of Grey Owl and Anahareo for
many years.

Hope and her husband cared for an injured beaver in their
home; it had been injured in some unknown way. Hope
had nursed it back to good health and it had become as
tame as Jelly Roll. We were able to pick it up, and Dawn
and I took turns  holding it in our arms. With
the beaver cuddled close to us we posed for photos. Hope
wrote about our visit in the next release of the magazine,
*"The Beaver Defenders."*

Our visit with Hope and her husband became favorite memories, as we related to her kindness towards wildlife and her great understanding respect for the denizens of wilderness areas. Another highlight of our 1976 travel, after bidding farewell to the Beaver Defenders was travelling west across the United States. We were able to visit the highlights of many areas along the way; Kansas City, Denver, Colorado; Salt Lake City, then across the Utah Salt Flats before heading north to Canada, and returning home to Kamloops.

After this five-week journey, the odometer on our camper showed we had travelled approximately 8000 miles. I calculated our gasoline costs for this trip and learned it cost us five cents per mile. We'd seen a lot of country and had met with many interesting people along the way, for a total gasoline cost of $400.00.

Later in the summer of 1976, another relative of Dawn's was about to enter our life. She received a phone call from Leonard Scott-Brown, her uncle, who was living in Vancouver. Leonard had just come back from visiting Gertie in Victoria and, concerned that he'd found her not feeling well, immediately phoned Dawn upon his arrival home. As he wanted Dawn to know about her mother, he had asked Gertie for our phone number.

When Dawn immediately contacted her Mom, she tried to persuade Gertie to come to Kamloops to live. Her difficulties living in Victoria were increasing, especially as there was a long stairway to get up to her suite. As Gertie was not too interested in making the move, Dawn and I went to Victoria a week later on our days off.

When we arrived, we found Gertie quite happy, greeting us as welcomed visitors. She was obviously feeling quite well by this time, and she kept letting us know how happy she was to be living in Victoria. We joined her for a small drink of wine. We recognized Gertie was being very independent and happy; she was seventy years of age. She did a dance around her little living room, then suddenly flipped a cartwheel completely over her coffee table, landing upright on her feet. Then she laughed.

We recognized she was about as happy as one could be. We stayed with her, shared coffee with her and more visiting. Dawn and I decided she was capable of taking care of herself, although we were pleased she did agree to think about relocating to Kamloops by the time we left for home. A few weeks later she decided to relocate and a mobile home was purchased in a trailer park in Kamloops.

In the meantime, Dawn had spoken a number of times to Leonard Scott-Brown in Vancouver. He was a half-brother to Archie Belaney, Grey Owl, and had apparently come to Canada in the early 1930`s as an employee of the Hudson Bay Company. He had been stationed in Aklavik, high up in Canada`s Arctic.

Soon we actually enjoyed a visit when Leonard and his good wife Florence came up to Kamloops for the wedding of Dawn`s daughter Sandra. We found Leonard to be very interesting; a man we enjoyed talking with and visiting. Leonard`s experiences were broad.

In 1932, when the RCMP tracked the Mad Trapper, Albert Johnson, then shot him on the Yukon River in February 1932, Leonard was a member of the Inquest Board into the killing. He`d been stationed in Aklavik at that time, one of the number of places where Leonard had lived while with the HBC . He`d also been at Tuktoyaktuk, Herschel Island, and as far east as Moosonee on the Southern tip of James Bay.

Dawn had known her father had a younger half-brother but thought he was still somewhere in England. His coming into our life began a very close association with Dawn and me. We frequently visited with Leonard and Florence in their Vancouver home, and it became like a second home for us; our home in Vancouver.We visited Leonard and Florence in Vancouver a number of times during the winter 1976, and spring of 1977.

Leonard treated Dawn like a father and she savoured his affection. After all, his mother and Archie`s was Kitty Cox, Dawn`s grandmother. We learned from Leonard, that in 1939, when war was a threat in Europe, he left the Hudson Bay Company to return to his English birth place and to join the British army. He served through the war with the British army in North Africa, Italy and through Europe, then stayed on with the Occupation

Forces after the war ended. He returned to Canada in 1950. He left the British Army as a Lieutenant Colonel. After arriving in Canada, he met and married Florence, a Canadian nurse.

Early spring Dawn and I made a number of short trips within British Columbia to various lakes and camping areas. Dawn came up with thoughts that it would be nice for her mother, along with Leonard, to take a journey to Beaver Lodge. Gertie had never been back there since she left Archie in 1936, and Leonard had never visited the spot where his famous half-brother had spent his final years.

This journey needed planning, as we would have to collaborate with Parks Canada to take us to Lake Ajawaan. It would be a long journey for one day. After we determined that both Leonard and Gertie would agree to our plans, communication with the Park was started. We would take the trip as early as possible during the next summer.

Dawn wrote letters to Parks Canada and the final arrangements were made for the trip to take place in June. It was decided Leonard and Gertie would travel together in Leonard`s car and we would travel with our camper van, meeting them in Waskesiu on a specific day. When June 1977 arrived, our travel plans were still holding and we were all ready for the historical journey.

The day we gathered at the Park`s office we met with Merv Syroteuk, who was eager to transport us and had

arranged for two Park`s boats  for transportation.  A
canoe would also be taken for use on Lake Ajawaan.

The canoe was brought for Leonard and Gertie along with
Merv, to cross the expanse of Lake Ajawaan to the
cabin at the North end of the lake. It was a canoe journey
which Anahareo had made many times, not only with
Grey Owl, but also on her own. We were aware what a
dramatic and an historical event it would be.

We left the Park Office in Waskesiu shortly after eight in
the morning,  and drove to the landing at the South end of
Lake Kingsmere.  We were using two Park`s boats to take
us across; Gertie, Leonard, Dawn and I, rode in one with
Merv, and the second boat carried the Park`s
staff, who were towing the canoe. As we headed
northward. the lake was calm  that morning as it
frequently was. Yet at times, in late afternoons it could
shake the life out of a boat along with everyone in it.
It could be a treacherous lake if one was caught in
carelessness and didn`t know its characteristics. Gertie
and Archie knew the lake and what it could do at times.

During our calm crossing northward I could see Gertie
fidgeting in her excitement. I tried to imagine the  thoughts
which must have been going through her mind.  Forty
years had passed since she had made the decision to leave
Archie behind for good.

After we arrived at the north end of Kingsmere and
reorganized, Merv packed the canoe on the half-mile
portage to the south end of Lake Ajawaan. We all walked

down to the shoreline, then helped as Merv settled
Leonard and Gertie in the canoe. Dawn and I again
started the rest of the hike along the meandering pathway
towards the cabin. We again felt the spirits of wilderness
along the Aspen-lined pathway. We had just arrived at the
cabin, when Leonard, Gertie and Merv arrived and pulled
the canoe up on shore.

Merv and another Park gentleman had their cameras
ready to take a few historical snaps. Gertie walked slowly
towards the open door of the cabin, obviously with
apprehension, because she knew the cabin was lifeless.
As she peered through the open doorway her eyes filled
with a rush of tears and her only comment was, *"No more
Jelly Roll!"* She paused motionless for what seemed the
longest time. It had been forty years since she and Archie,
and their wee Dawn, had all been there together. Her life
and memories were running full circle. All was quiet as
we stood silently, and realized this lady was the one who
influenced Archie away from his killing and trapping life,
and turned him into the protector of wildlife and
specifically the beaver.

He had learned to nurture them, play with them, respect
them and love them, and told the rest of the world to pay
attention and regard them as *"little people."* Gertie had
been the leader of Archie`s cause, even though they
couldn`t stay together, she had defended him in spirit
for the rest of her life.

This grey-haired lady stood spellbound as she reminisced
to herself. I realized we were participating in the making

of a part of Canadian History. Gertie had her memories, and Leonard now understood the epitome of his half-brother`s life. I held Dawn`s hand gently, as I understood the privilege I was experiencing in life. The Spirit of the Wilderness had drawn Dawn and me closer and closer, and I felt all of this had been predetermined by someone greater than ourselves, and that all in life was meant to be.

We travelled in convoy back to Kamloops. Leonard spent another three or four days with us before leaving for home in Vancouver. After that, Dawn and I took short trips around BC, and camped at various lakes, to sit by a fire and not only reminisce our travel to Beaver Lodge, but to grow closer in our understanding of each other.

I knew now how much Dawn had dedicated her whole adult life to raising and preserving the image of her parents, towards their beliefs and Dawn`s belief, that the Wilderness of Canada, along with all the denizens of the forest, needed the protection and consideration by all of us for future generations.She was a spiritual reincarnation of her father`s goals, and her mother`s hopes.

Later in the summer of 1977 Dawn and I camped in the Forest Service campground at Knouff Lake. This lake was thirty miles from Kamloops, and at an elevation of 4000 feet. It was a quiet and peaceful area, where the spruce and fir trees were sixty feet high. The loons called as they majestically floated by, and the Whiskey Jacks were fluttering around our campsite looking for a treat, searching for whatever we might have left out for them. Our neat bonfire was crackling satisfactorily, and the aroma of a fresh pot of coffee brewing on the fire, added to our contentment as we relaxed our weary bones.

When the coffee was just right, we added our traditional touch of brandy, and rested comfortably on our camp chairs, talking and reminiscing about our past travels, and of the things we dreamed of doing in the future. Both of us were aware that we were commencing another chapter of our life together. We wanted our plans to be sure, and that we'd be making them within a short time.

We were awakened by the loons calling in the early morning. With the morning sun shining upon the calm lake, and the reflection of the tall, thin spruce trees of a small island a few hundred feet out from shore, we arose to be greeted by a perfect photo image; not a ripple of the water disturbing it.

After breakfast, having enjoyed a newly percolated pot of coffee and some toast with wild raspberry jam which Dawn had made to treat our taste buds, we packed up for a drive, planning to sight-see around the area. At the south end of the lake, were two or three cabins which had been built on subdivided lots. We drove around the area for a while, then stopped when we spotted a private "For Sale" sign nailed to a tree alongside of the main road.

We got out of our van without either of us speaking a word, and walked around on the secluded property. I was immediately thinking, "why can`t we make this place into our future home?" We rested together on an old fir stump three feet in diameter, and sat in complete silence. Our seat was only part of the forest. This area had been logged in the 1940`s, and second growth trees surrounding us were now towering at least sixty feet up into the sky.

As I gazed at the layout of the land which sloped slightly in the direction of the lake, I visualized a large cedar home with a big wood stove, and a studio large enough for both Dawn and me to work in comfortably. I imagined the smell of fresh coffee percolating every morning, the fire crackling in the wood stove on a winter morning, snow hanging precariously from the eaves of the roof, creating a picture postcard for us.

When I asked Dawn if we should check on what dollars they were asking for the property, she just smiled. I knew I could build our house, as in previous years I had built two homes. Enthusiasm was creeping up on both of us, we were tired of renting and had already been recognizing a home of our own would be nice. A few days later, after much discussion, we made an offer on the property. To our surprise the offer was accepted. We were now joint owners of a beautiful lot secluded amongst the tall spruce, fir and balsam at Knouff Lake.
We immediately cleared a parking area for our van on this new lot of ours, and I built a picnic table and

outdoor toilet. We now had our own property to camp on whenever we wished.

Later in the fall Dawn left the secretarial pool. She'd been hired by the Federal Government Manpower office, as she had worked some years prior for the Federal Government at Dawson Creek, B.C. It was an active year. Then we moved out of our apartment and purchased a mobile home in a trailer park located in downtown Kamloops, along the South Thompson River. Now we were property owners and home owners.

During the early winter months, we talked about building our dream home at Knouff Lake. If we wished, we could start in the spring, I thought. I started drawing our house plans while we discussed, thought about and planned what style of home would best suit us. We finally decided we wanted a two-storey cedar frame home with a spiral stairway and a big wood stove.

I went to OK Builders for a cost estimate of the construction material required. By doing the work ourselves we projected we could build the place for twenty thousand. Added to this, of course, would be the initial property costs, as well as the expense of a drilled well and septic field. With our two incomes, it looked as though we would have no problem raising that amount whenever we made the final decision to proceed.

I still have the blueprints I had made of our home to be. As far as architectural blueprints are concerned, particularly for the Regional District, there were numerous points of structural details I had left out. But, back then the basic construction of foundation and framing shown on my blueprints met with the approval of the Regional District Inspector, and he accepted the plans along with my $75.00 cheque to cover the building permit. I sat down with Dawn again and asked the question: " Are we going to go ahead with our dreams and build our own home?" She nodded with approval.

In the spring of 1978, I learned there was a man with a dozer working in the Knouff Lake area. I asked him to come over and please level our building site. A few days later, he cleared and levelled the area which I had staked out. When Dawn and I went up to our property after this was done and she saw the cleared patch of land, she broke into tears. *"Where have all the trees gone?"* she demanded, crying broken heartedly. *"You have destroyed all the trees."* With some difficulty I convinced her to walk around the property with me and let me show her the actual area that was needed for our home.

Although we both had drawn the plans for it she had not realized how much the property had to change to accommodate the construction. I tried to explain that we must have a septic field dug and a well drilled. *"Once it is built,"* I said, hoping to relieve her concerns necessitating the removal of the trees, *"the trees will be close to the house and our big cedar home will be nicely secluded."*

She felt I had stripped the property; she was furious!. I didn`t know whether or not she was going to tell me to go to hell, and to plan on living in the secluded shack by myself. What a predicament! Surely, I thought, I hoped she would eventually see just what is taking place and I wouldn`t have to abandon all the plans we had made. The tension in our home was heavy for a few days.

The next time we returned together to our Knouff Lake property, and after walking the place again, she calmed her spirits. It seemed she`d accepted where we were going in life, although I wasn`t feeling over-confident about all this taking place. But I had no choice, other than to tip-toe forward in life with her, and hope for the best.

In retrospect, I realize how much she had wanted to be present when the man with the dozer came, but that wasn`t possible. We were both at work that day when the dozer operator cleared the land. There were more struggles related to our home building together to come in the future.

Chapter 4

We built a ten-by-twelve cabin in the early spring 1978, that would be our summer accommodation while we were building the main house.

It was cozy, as we'd purchased an old wood cook stove. It was in good condition and had a water reservoir as well as a warming oven. We built bench seats and a drop-leaf table that converted into a bed. We were comfortable in our little cabin, I thought, recognizing what a good guest house it would become later.

We had an old utility trailer that I'd hitch to the van, and we'd take it and my new chain saw into the bush and gather trees for firewood. Dawn was enthusiastic as we worked together. Our future looked promising! We had to drive into town daily for work, and could work only evenings and weekends on our property until our holiday time.

I hoped to have the sub floor finished by early July, so we worked until dusk every evening. Then we'd have our kerosene lamp dinners, usually with a shot of brandy or a glass of good dry red wine, finally retiring after a long day's work. Building a house is a massive task, especially with the two of us wanting to create the whole project by ourselves.

After OK Builders delivered our first load of material, we immediately started on the big job ahead of us. When I had footing-forms built with rebar in them, we ordered the concrete. After the footings were poured from the big ready-mix truck, and the concrete had set, the sub floor would rest upon three rows of cement building blocks. For that job, Dawn hand-mixed the cement in a wheelbarrow while I put the blocks in place. At this stage, she was enthusiastic as Jelly Roll, and we continued compatibly building our new home on the mountain.

When the sub floor was complete, the framing with pre-cut 2X6 studs went up quickly. After the framing was completed for the first level, we started construction on the second storey. Dawn's son Glaze helped to raise the sheeted wall sections as they were built. By early October the place was at lock-up stage, with all windows and doors installed.

Proud of our achievement, we took a break from it all and went to Vancouver for a long weekend to visit Dawn's Uncle Leonard, and Aunt Florence. Leonard decided to come up for a few days to help us with some work. He relished his stay in the cabin, while Dawn and I used our camper van for sleeping. Early mornings found Dawn frying bacon and eggs on the old wood stove, as the coffee pot scented the air, making the atmosphere ideal for a good breakfast. That, plus the toast with Dawn's wild raspberry jam, were memories of the place which Leonard never forgot.

By the end of October the nights were getting frosty, even for us in the cabin, as the wood cook stove didn't hold enough heat to keep us warm through the night. When the water pail began to have a skim of ice in the morning, we decided it would soon be time to move back to the city for winter.

It was during one of those last nights we planned to stay up at the lake, that Dawn experienced heavy chest pains. Her diabetes again had flared and was taking a toll on her health. Another problem she was experiencing was one with her vision. On our way into the hospital during the middle of the night, I began to question our project, and I began wondering if we should abandon our building plans.

When we arrived at the Emergency ward, Dawn was wheeled in immediately. A short time later, I sat beside her hospital bed where she was on oxygen. Two days later she was discharged and we had some quiet days in our mobile home, where we talked a lot about the plans we had made and our Knouff Lake project. We'd learned that apparently Dawn's heart condition was not severe.

Most of the heavy work we had faced was almost complete, and we recognized that we both wanted the house. We yearned for its atmosphere knowing we'd both be happy then.We worked weekends for the balance of the winter, now at a more relaxed pace. I did the inside insulation and sheeting, not too difficult for me to do much of it alone. Dawn was feeling great again, and her enthusiasm and determination showed with every step we achieved. As we kept working I again felt at ease, especially more when I saw Dawn determined to achieve a lifestyle that we both could visualize and so much wanted.

When the spring of 1979 arrived we were back up on the mountain and living in our cabin by April. I did the drywall taping, interior trims around the windows and doors, and tiled the floor of our second-storey studio room, as well as the smaller bedroom. Then I worked on the downstairs living room, where the big wood stove would be.

I enjoyed building the wall directly behind where the stove would sit, covering it with decorative brick from floor to ceiling. The stove would rest on squares of black slate, grouted with cement, complimenting the living room and dining area flooring that was to be dark oak parquet. The kitchen, or course, would be tiled as was the half-bathroom downstairs. Our home was coming together.

One day while I was struggling with some wall-to-wall carpet, trying to get it upstairs to install in our bedroom, Dawn came over to help me lift it up the spiral stairway. Chest pains struck her! With deep sadness I realized again just what years of diabetes could do to one's general health, as we rushed her to the hospital with another heart attack.

Dawn was only 46; I was 50. I was feeling overwhelmed, wondering what was really in store for us in life. As I sat beside her bed in hospital a couple of days later, I could see colour was back in her cheeks, and she was on her feet again. I puzzled about our situation. This was the lady I had learned to love so much, and I was at odds with myself.

I began to blame myself for coaxing her along to achieve our dreams together, and was worrying that perhaps they were not meant to be. I had to keep working to finish the place. As I worked, I struggled desperately within myself and all the thoughts and reasons why we started this project in the first place. Neither one of us enjoyed city life as much as rural places, and especially wilderness atmospheres. We both felt a great sense of comfort beneath the stars and tall trees, perhaps because our youth and a portion of our beginnings conditioned us that way.

With Dawn`s roots as the daughter of world-recognized Conservationists, Grey Owl and Anahareo, and my upbringing in rural Northwestern Ontario, the feeling of being together in the fresh outdoors atmosphere gave both of us a sense of comfort. We both believed what her father said, " *We belong to Nature; not it to us.*"

It was mid-life for both of us, and we both felt a new turn in life for us would be rewarding, as we experienced a call of the wild along with the beckoning of tall timber around us. It had to be good for both of us, because the dreams we were sharing was a comfort to both of us, I felt.I finished the floors, then created a wood box on the end north wall, adjacent to where the stove would sit. I cut an opening through the wall to the outside exterior, closing it with an insulated door, which would allow us to place firewood in the house from outside.

As it was her second heart attack, Dawn was kept in hospital for a week so she could be monitored. I realized her courage each time I visited, and we talked about our home and its progress. When she was discharged she was back to her old self again. At the end of July, 1979 we moved in to our new cedar home, achieving that part of our dream.

Fall came and Dawn was feeling well, and I had cut enough firewood in the logged areas several miles beyond Knouff Lake, to carry us through our first winter. I felt grateful that we had achieved this step. Even though we were settled in our new home, we were not quite the couple we wanted to be; we were not yet married.

After we talked it over we set our wedding day for October 15, 1979. We decided we would marry in the house we had built by hand. Almost single-handedly, and without electricity, as BC Hydro would not complete the power line until the spring of 1980.

We arranged for Reverend Pederson from the Kamloops United Church to come up and perform the wedding ceremony in our living room. In addition to our family members, we invited thirty guests. Mrs. Winters travelled from Saskatchewan to be with us, and Donald Smith, Professor of History at the University of Calgary joined us.

He was a special guest as he had grown to know us as he spent years researching details about Dawn`s father, Grey Owl, in preparation for his forthcoming book, *"From The Land of Shadows."*

My brother, James and his wife Dorothy, came up from Vernon, B.C and James was best man. Dawn`s daughter, Sandra was bridesmaid, and Anahareo proudly came down the spiral stairway with Dawn as the lady to give Dawn unto the ceremony. Dawn`s son Glaze escorted young Grey, Sandra`s son, Dawn`s grandson, with the rings. The music of Placido Domingo played softly in the background.

Dawn wore a full-length skirt of forest green aboriginal designs, a white blouse and an aboriginal designed shawl. Gertie had dark slacks, a burgundy blouse and a buckskin vest with bead work. I purchased a new dark grey suit for the occasion. Outside, the scattered Aspen, a few small birch trees and the alder bushes, displayed their beauty of fall gold, orange and yellow. I had designed our own wedding invitations with a photo of our hand-built home on the front fold, and inside I wrote the following words:

*We stand alone in solitude,*
*Beneath majestic pine;*
*Their movement gently beckons us,*
*To join with Nature`s rhyme;*
*To join together hand in hand,*
*In Nature throughout life,*
*To stand together hand in hand,*
*To stand as husband and wife.*

Married, we now went on with our life, ready for our first winter in our new home.

Because of Dawn's fragile health, she was offered a disability retirement from Manpower by the Federal Government. She accepted it. Dawn felt quite well during the winter, and we lived quietly enjoying our kerosene-lit dinners. Then in March of 1980, B.C. Hydro connected the power, and we celebrated with light bulbs glowing throughout the house.

Again, I was feeling the stress from almost 35 years with CN as rail traffic controller. Even when Dawn and I were together, during all our travels and especially during the hard work building our home, I had been facing growing concerns within myself about my job. I had been assigned to controlling the train movements between Vancouver and Kamloops since arriving here in 1968, from Ontario.

The Fraser Canyon where the rails wind like ribbons around the curves and on the rocky ledges beside the Fraser River, and through a number of tunnels, is a treacherous piece of track. The snow and rock slides of January, February and March were the norm for many shifts that I worked. Work gangs repairing tracks and clearing slides had to be looked after amongst all the train traffic. Safety was primary, and we worked hard to create it and maintain it. The stress of the years of it all, seemed to be getting worse. One loses tolerance on a job like that, particularly when the thirty-five year mark was looking me straight in my face. With Dawn now on a pension, I was 52 years old and was beginning to want out. Burn-out as it`s referred to, and I had it.

I had hired as a Morse operator in Port Arthur, Ontario in 1945, when I was 17. I felt I had served my time. I applied for a disability pension not knowing what would happen. I had no idea of what I would receive for income; I just knew that I wanted out. With Dawn`s health being very fragile, I wanted us to have time together; time to do some travelling. I hoped to be able to achieve years of a more relaxed lifestyle with her.

My last shift of work with CN was May 26, 1980. My pensions came through higher than what I had projected. Now we were together with two retirement incomes. Our world was ours and we were happy. Dawn was still having regular health checks, but we were free of the stress of previous years.

Whatever life we had ahead of us we looked forward to it. Between the short travel periods we took around the Interior of B.C., I started to do more painting than I had ever done before. Dawn was working on a book. She had become upset with the strychnine poisoning of wolves, and with the helicopter shooting of them as well. She refused to accept that wolves were becoming over-populated and detrimental to local ranchers.

Again she believed that was inaccurate, that wolves had little chance of escaping their image as vicious killers simply because generations of human population had been conditioned to think of them, as through the Fairy Tale " *Little Red Ridinghood*."

After speaking with most of the local ranchers, she learned that less than 1% of livestock were victims of wolf attacks. I can still visualize her sitting at her desk in our upstairs studio working on her writing, as I was at my easel working on a painting. We were finally experiencing in our home, doing what each of us liked to do together.

Gertie would come up to visit us and often wanted to stay by herself in our cabin guest house. Kerosene lamps, the wood crackling in the stove, and coffee purcolating, pleasantly reminded her of when she and Archie travelled the wilderness of Quebec and Northern Ontario. She was happy in the cabin  with all her memories.

The Federation of Canadian Artists were organizing in town. Following their approval of samples of my work I took out membership.  The FCA had their own gallery in Vancouver down in the gas-town area. It consisted of two exhibition rooms which artists could rent for short-term exhibitions. I decided to have a show of my paintings in the big city.

For the  openning,  I displayed twenty-five of my oils for one week. Dawn and I stayed with Leonard and Florence, although most of the time I was at my exhibition.  I sold several works as the result of my show and felt good about it.

Dawn and I wanted Gertie to feel welcome to visit us at our mountain home, we decided we had to be firm about her not drinking while she was up there. We told her no booze, as the ground was rough and could be dangerous for her at her age. We wanted her to have a quiet visit, welcome to stay in the cabin for as long as she wished

I went into town one morning to pick her up and bring her home. Dawn didn`t come with me on this trip, as she had work she wanted to get done. I picked Gertie up at her mobile home. She was ready and waiting and seemed ok. When we were driving through town, I usually made it a point to avoid going by the liquor stores. Gertie knew how to tease seriously and had a nose for good whiskey.

When I turned on to the by-pass she demanded:
*"Where in hell are ye going Bob?*
*"Up the mountain to our place!"* I replied.
*"Let`s take a short detour...I`d like a bottle of wine!"*
she said casually.
*"No , no ,"* I replied.
*"You know what our thoughts are. We don`t want you to get hurt up there, or burn the cabin down, or fall on the rocks."*

Gertie slid quietly to the edge of the truck seat, and slowly wound the window down as we drove down a main street. Suddenly she opened the truck door and stood out on the running board. What the hell was she up to? I thought! With some panic as I tried to slow down. She began hollering:
*"Help, help! I`m being kidnapped!"*

She kept screaming those words.
"*Jesus Christ, get back into this truck,*" I shouted!
"*Fuck you!*" Gertie hollered, as I gently pushed on the
brake pedal. Then she slowly moved back on to the seat,
and closed the truck door. As she turned to face me, I
could see her eyes sparkling as she began to laugh loudly.
"*You win!* " She conceded.
"*But it`s only because we are on your territory,*" she
explained. All was quiet again. Believe it, Gertie knew
how to dig at people!

However, I really can`t remember a serious argument
between us. We respected each other, and Dawn`s Mom
and I were friends for life. I did resolve that I wouldn`t
pick her up on my own again. And I recognized
thankfully, that Dawn`s humour was much more subtle.

Chapter 5

Gertie would often come up to our mountain home to visit. In the summer months she always insisted on her private time in the cabin, which worked well with Dawn`s and my working on our projects of writing and painting. She would have her morning coffee and breakfast by herself, and would join us in the house for lunch and supper.

During the evenings Dawn and I could see the kerosene lamp flickering and knew Gertie was reading at the little table, close to the lamp and happy to be all by herself in the cabin. She liked it that way. I learned much, chatting with Gertie, and learned about Archie as well. Never once did I ever hear her drag his behaviour and character down.

Yet their relationship had been on and off, probably because of their eighteen years age difference, and because of his constant writing which was his passion. Gertie explained Archie was nocturnal and he would sit up and write...scratch...scratch...scratch all night long. Then he would lay on the bunk of the cabin and sleep most of the day. His young Mohawk wife became increasingly isolated from him, and missed their outings. This incompatibility grew between them.

Gertie said Archie was a gentleman, very modest in her presence, understandably with his childhood background of being raised by his two strict aunts in Hastings, England. Archie could hold his own amongst the best of bushmen, but he was a somewhat loner in his life, and

Gertie delighted in his ability to be a prankster, and a humorous dare-devil; he was her Jessie James.

Gertie was also a prankster; I certainly learned that about her myself. They also both liked their booze. Sometimes they had fun with it, sometimes they didn`t. Although Dawn and I shared many glasses of wine or sips of brandy, and we had our disagreement occasionally. Archie got the character assassination for his prankster behaviour. But it seems to me at least some of it, were exaggerations; the price one pays by some folks for fame, or perhaps being aboriginal. I was grateful that our life was peaceful. At this point in our lives together, Dawn`s children had grown up. Sandra and Glaze were out on their own and both doing well.

Gertie, as Anahareo, had been awarded recognition for her work and talks on Conservation, by The International League for The Rights of Animals. She accepted the Honour at a large gathering at Vancouver`s Hyatt Regency. Dawn, myself and Sandra and many others enjoyed watching her graciously accept. She was also presented Honours by the City of Kamloops for her work and times with Grey Owl. And there would be more honours to come.

With Dawn being a daughter of famous parents, we had numerous visitors to our home on the mountain. One was a Toronto film producer who was considering creating a TV mini-series about Archie and Gertie. Another producer took an option on Grey Owl`s book: *"The Adventures of Sajo and The Beaver People."*

There were others who wanted to visit and to hear
first-hand stories about Grey Owl and Anahareo`s life
together. They wanted to hear about the beavers, about
how Dawn had romped and played with Rawhide and
Jelly Roll.

These people were welcome to come and speak with
Dawn. She found chatting with them a spiritual
incarnation for both of her parents. Dawn had the same
philosophy as these famous Conservationists. Her mother
had once been criticized by outdoors people as being a
bleeding heart. To this she explained: *"I`m just for the
beaver, the wildlife, the trees. People should be educated
about them, as animals are more human than a lot of
people."*

Dawn and I purchased a Sportspal canoe... a fourteen
foot, it weighing only 45 pounds. It was suitable for us
because of its wide beam and oar locks so we could either
row or paddle. The canoe was on top of our van. Gertie
didn`t think too much of it when she first saw
it. *"That`s a mutation!"* She said indignantly.
*"No it`s not... it`s a good canoe for us."* I stated
passively. *"It`s unsinkable, it`s sturdy, it has foam seats,
and we can sit comfortably in it for the whole day,"* I
added. *"It`s a lazy man`s canoe!"* She summarized
critically.

We ended the discussion, as I could see she felt it was not
the type of canoe she would want to use, and she wasn`t
keen on it for her daughter`s image. In her younger days,
she could handle a canoe just as well as

Archie. She could throw a knife accurately, and handle a rifle as well. But Dawn and my world was different than hers.

We now had a Toyota Landcruiser for the winter months on the mountain. That thing could almost climb a tree and we had fun with it. Since Knouff Lake was good for ice fishing, and the January ice could be two feet thick, I'd drive out on the ice and fish in comfort in our Toyota. We would take a thermos of hot, black coffee, laced with a little brandy. Then when we got our limit of Kamloops trout pan fries, we would be back home again in five minutes and Dawn would cook us a big feed.

Remembering our seasons together often relates to our outings in that little Landcruiser. It had a Warren winch on the front . Dawn's job was to handle the remote control for the winch cable when we went for our winter firewood. We would travel up to the logging areas. I would be the hook-up man and we would drag trees from the slash piles. Then Dawn would drag the sucker right up to the vehicle with the winch. Then I'd buck it into stove lengths and load it into our utility trailer. We found it refreshing to be out in the woods and active. Since there were only two other families living in that area of the mountain at the time, firewood was easy to get, particularly as the logging contractors left a lot of wasted trees behind.

Our first winter passed quickly. I accomplished a lot of paintings, and Dawn worked on her book.

She had moments of difficulty with her writing, as she often felt her father was looking over her shoulder. His recognition as a writer and conservationist intimidated her at times, yet I felt she excelled as a writer with how she could handle the story. I often thought it must be an inherited trait.

By the fall of 1982, I was acting as her representative, sending her manuscript to some of the major publishers. A waiting game, as publisher responses are traditionally slow, but I felt there would be a definite need for her story in the future. Her book passionately and clearly explained the need for all wildlife, and why she abhorred the use of poisoning allowed for human control of animals. Her writing, her spirit and determination, reinforced the beliefs of her famous parents. I felt she did well, and would be recognized for her beliefs in the years to come.

While Dawn`s health was controlled by medication for angina and kidney problems, she was holding very well and with a good level of energy. We realized we may be able to take the journey planned for 1983. Our goal was to travel to Eastern Canada, as she wanted to visit as many places as possible where her mother and father had lived during their early years. It had been as trappers, then as protectors of the beaver following Archie`s first lectures in Metis, Quebec.

We`d made short trips during the winter months of 1982 and 1983 to Vancouver for visits with Uncle Leonard and Aunt Florence, and had spent Christmas 1982 with them. Leonard had become like a father to Dawn, and we were warmly welcomed in their home. Similarly we welcomed family and friends to our mountain home.

It was warm in our well-insulated house, and comfortable. Dawn would frequently stand behind our big wood stove, looking out the front window at the winter`s beauty and tranquillity. We fed Whiskey Jacks, Chickadees, Steller`s Jays and Squirrels on the exterior ledge of our living room window, watching them flutter and hop. We loved our environment dearly, as our guests did, especially Anahareo.Without wine, she was much more that name than Gertie. Dawn and I were content in our world.

If the snow was not too deep along the old logging roads beyond where we lived, we would sometimes drive five miles up into the bush to Little Badger Lake. It took a four-wheel drive to get up there, even during summer and early fall. Dawn didn`t enjoy driving those roads during the fall hunting season. She couldn`t face the killing of wildlife, and became upset if we happened to come across hunters dressing a killed deer. Whereas most hunters make it a practice not to flaunt their kill, on one occasion we came face-to-face with two hunters who had hung a buck deer from a large lower branch of a Douglas fir.

They were gutting it right beside the road prior to loading it into their pick-up.*"Stop this friggen jeep,"* she demanded. She jumped out and bellowed,

*"Why do you idiots do this right along the roadway?"* as
she glanced at them. They gazed sheepishly at her and
said nothing. She got back into the Landcruiser, tears
flowing. It was difficult for her, and she was right. They
could have cleaned the buck back in the trees off the road.

We also had other adventures on our back roads. We
were amazed to learn how some people would drive into
the outback on the old logging roads, not knowing where
they were going, nor whether or not they could get their
vehicle turned around to go back home.

One Sunday afternoon in late fall, we were driving an
abandoned road, and we came across an elderly couple
standing beside their car. They were deep in the bush,
four miles away from any help, something they obviously
hadn't considered should they have car trouble. They
were dressed in light jackets and were wearing unsuitable
low loafers on their feet.

Once they realized how far they were from any homes,
they had attempted to turn around and head back out. He
had backed his car only a few feet off the travelled portion
of the old logging road, when the rear wheels suddenly
sank into a small water and mud hole. Their vehicle stuck
solid. They were in serious trouble, as it was late
afternoon. It would be a tough hike out, even if
they were capable of walking the four miles to the nearest
help. How glad they were that we happened to come
along. Fortunately for them, we had the Landcruiser's
Warren winch and began pulling them

out.We got them out, turned around, then followed them to ensure their safety back to the main road.

Dawn and I knew to use caution and common sense when travelling far into the backwoods. We always dressed well, including our good walking boots, and carried cans of fresh fruit juice in a small pack along with us. During the fall periods when it could be cold at night, we carried the usual survival gear, so that we always were able to cope if something happened to the Landcruiser.

By spring of 1983, I was developing far more as an artist, probably because of Dawn`s perceptive support. I had arranged for a small art show in the Museum, Riding Mountain National Park. It was scheduled for July, before we continued east to Quebec.

The same spring brought great news. It was happy for all of us, especially exciting for Anahareo. She was to receive The Order of Canada for her Conservation work. She was being recognized for talks she gave for schools and clubs, as well as for her support of Archie Belaney, Grey Owl. We felt she had well-earned it, as she had been the lady who transformed Archie from trapper to conservationist, and both of them received world recognition. Because Gertie`s health was becoming fragile, Governor General Edward Schruyer, who was in B.C. at the end of June, came to Kamloops to honour Anahareo.

Along with fifty invited guests, we gathered in the Chambers of Kamloops City Hall for the occasion. Anahareo stood proudly before the Governor General, her silver hair highlighted her outfit. She'd chosen to wear a burgundy blouse, a buckskin vest and black slacks. She was accompanied by Glaze, six-foot-two grandson, who had blue eyes like his grandfather. We were proud as Anahareo received The Order of Canada. Later we recognized that our Gertie had accepted the reward with humility.

A few days after the ceremony, Dawn and I packed our van and headed East. We had planned we would go as far as Metis Beach, Quebec, located on the Southern shore of the St. Lawrence River on the Gaspe.

Our first major stop-over would be in The Riding Mountain National Park's Pinewood Museum, where I would set up my work. The paintings were to be left hanging there, to be picked up again on our homeward journey. As we drove out from our mountain home we recognized how excited we were that Anahareo became the recipient of The Order of Canada, and now we were leaving on our much hoped-for journey to Quebec.

As soon as we arrived at the Riding Mountain Park, we visited with Emma Ringstrom and her husband. Then we set up camp in the Park campground. We received a warm welcome from Ron Routledge, the Chief Naturalist, who had previously invited me to show my work in the Interpretative Centre. We stayed there two days then headed eastward again for a short stop in

Winnipeg, then on to Thunder Bay. Following three days visiting there with family and relatives, we headed east towards Grey Owl country again, into a new area of experience for both of us.

Dawn's father had trapped during his early years around the Cochrane, Ontario area, where he'd also worked as a Forest Ranger. Dawn knew that her father had been north to Moosonee on the Southern tip of James Bay, and she was pleased to be going there as well.

Our first evening, we were in a campground by Lake Helen in the Nipigon area. Resting by our bonfire, we chatted for a time of restful conversation, anticipating our days ahead. We would board, in Cochrane, the Ontario Northland Polar Bear Express to Moosonee. We were both looking forward to seeing a small part of Canada's North, as not only was it the area where her father worked, but Uncle Leonard had been stationed at Moosonee with the Hudson Bay Company. We had heard many of his stories about it during our visits.

We camped in the Drury Campground at Cochrane and made arrangements to catch the North-bound train the following morning. At that time, Cochrane a town with a Northern atmosphere, had a population of approximately 5000. When I read Dawn's hand-written journal, I could visualize it again. Dawn described how most yards had several cords of clean birch firewood stacked near the house.

At 8:00a.m., on The Polar Bear Express we headed for
James Bay, Moosonee, then on to Moose Factory by
boat. As we headed north we watched the scrub spruce
getting smaller as we travelled. We saw the occasional
trapper`s cabin, located not too far from the railway line.
At some of those isolated homes, the rugged bush folks
waved their hands as we sped past. Even now, I can feel
how it was for us, to be heading into one of the small
parts of Canada`s North.

Arriving  Moosonee at noon, we wandered down the main
gravel street. In that immediate area, there were only a
few miles of road, and they were not subject to Ontario
Highway Laws and Regulations. Kids of any size and age
could drive the few vehicles there provided they could see
over the steering wheel. A nicely constructed hotel and
gift shop provided for The Polar Bear Express` 400
tourists that day, a usual number of visitors every summer.
We stopped for lunch before strolling down to the
waterfront. Although there was a
tour boat to take people over to the island where Moose
Factory was located, we chose to try and get a ride over
with an Indian in a big freighter canoe. We did find an
Indian to take us to Moose Factory.

At Moose Factory, there was a large hospital serving
much of the North, and a Federal Government Marine
Office. Dawn`s journal mentions the terrific erosion on the
banks of the island, caused by spring icebreak and
movement. She also recorded:

*"There were dozens of big freighter canoes going back and forth at full speed, and some of the Indians were standing up in them and waving cheerfully. These people were certainly catering to the tourist trade, and appeared to be doing well."*

Also in her notes, is the fact that during the winter months, when the ice becomes three or four feet thick, a winter road is maintained between Moosonee and the Island of Moose Factory. The natives at Moose Factory had a number of tepees set up and were cooking bannok, and selling gifts made of beads and furs. People there did not appear to be in as much of a rush, nor as aggressive as those running businesses on the mainland.

Dawn felt that the Indians at Moose Factory were not at all very talkative or interested, until we stepped into one large tepee where a lady was baking bannok. We had bannok and tea while we visited with this well-spoken lady. Before we left, she allowed me to take one photo.

In Moosonee, Dawn noted in her journal about their excellent Education and Cultural Centre. She felt their work constructing birch-bark canoes was very well displayed. Because of Dawn's being half Mohawk and having Native features, these people were willing to speak openly with her.

Following our supper that evening, we boarded the train for our return journey and arrived back in Cochrane at close to midnight. It had been a long day for us. We'd found it interesting and certainly a worthwhile trip. Now we could compare notes with Uncle Leonard when we got back home. Mind you, it had been in the late 1920`s; almost sixty years prior to our visit, when he`d been stationed at Moosonee.

Leaving Cochrane the next morning, we headed for Biscotasing, our next stop. From highway 11 south of Iroquois Falls, we took 101 to Timmins, then south on number 144 to Bisco. Archie`s early years had been spent trapping in the Bisco area. Archie first arrived in the Biscotasing area after spending his first years in Canada in the Temagami area and Bear Island. It was on the Bear Island Reserve that he`d been adopted by the people and had married his first wife Angele.

By the time Archie went to Bisco, he had learned their language and many of the Indian ways and cultural beliefs. But with his loner personality he`d become considered somewhat of a rebel. We`d talked about all this history as Dawn looked forward to walking in the area of her father`s footprints.

We drove the few miles in off highway 144 to the small village of Bisco, and found a campground near the lake. Tired from the day`s travelling from Cochrane, we settled in lawn chairs by a small fire as we sipped our welcomed coffee. We decided not to make any approaches to people about the topic of Grey Owl that day, realizing we had better wait until the following day.

From Dawn`s journal:

*"Bisco is a small settlement with the population scattered around the area, like cones which had fallen from the trees and just stayed there. There is one grocery store which serves as a Post Office and liquor vendor. Some of the residents have lived here all of their lives travelling to Sudbury on occasion to cash their cheques and buy groceries. There was no banking service for the population of about 50 people. The train stopped at Bisco and Bob took some pictures. The people still gather at the Railroad, just like the old days when my father was there. After months in the bush, my father must have been glad to see the houses of Bisco, which were scattered about like the pine cones."*

Out-croppings of the Pre Cambrian Shield snuggled along the lake edge. The lake was 22 miles long. When Dawn first saw it, she said *"Grey Owl brought recognition to this little town where the trees and the foliage hug the shore line."*

The next day her journal reads: *"Had a great visit with Libby and Lottie Sawyer, (72 and 92 years of age respectively). They remembered Archie drinking like everybody else did. He drank with Alex Espanial, and Bill Draper. Lottie said: ` There may be a knock on the door to ask if it was alright to have a dance at their house tonight.' One afternoon, Archie had asked if they could have a dance at their house if he brought the food. He brought special things like cake and cheese. "Archie was always a gentleman,"* Lottie added.

I could see the smile of appreciation on Dawn`s face.

She was always proud of her father, even though a few folks in our time preferred to see his character assassinated. Most had favorable comments to make, of course those few who didn`t had hurt Dawn. I was happy and felt very proud to be with her.

This area held many memories. It was where Archie met Marie Gerard, and their son Johnny was born in 1915. This son of Archie`s was raised by a friend of the community, Gordon Langevin`s parents. We met with them on our second day in Bisco. At first introduction after Dawn had told them who she was, we sensed an immediate coolness. But Dawn`s diplomatic approach soon softened their hearts and they invited us in for tea, and became warm and receptive . By the time we`d left, we learned that Archie had left Marie, not aware that she was pregnant.

Leaving Bisco for the New Liskard area, we camped a night there, The next day we crossed into Quebec, then north to Senneterre. We camped there savouring our traditional bonfire again. Gertie had often mentioned the town of Seneterre when chatting with Dawn and me, talking about having to move their trapping to Quebec, because of some closure for trapping areas in Ontario.

Now that he had this young Mohawk with him, Archie felt he had to trap for a living. I believe Gertie was Archie`s true love, a beauty he hoped to keep with him.
They travelled to Lake Simon where they planned to establish trap lines. This was also where  Gertie and

Archie were married by Chief Papati in 1926. This was a deep and solemn place in Dawn's thoughts, and we were soon to arrive there.

From Dawn's journal: *"At the end of a gravel road was the village of Lake Simon. Over a hundred inhabitants were living in houses, which were almost identical; most of which, in disrepair. The church and rectory however, are both in first class shape. There is a police detachment in the village manned by an Indian police force. People were sitting on their decks out in front of their homes. We spoke to two different men before being directed to the house of George Papati.*

*He was the great grandson of the Chief Papati, who had married my mother and father. Bob asked him about their Craft Shop. George said it could be open tomorrow, or Monday. If it wasn't it would be open the next day."*

As we drove down towards the lake, Dawn said she could almost visualize her mother and father, perhaps touching their hands as they disembark from their canoe.

We talked about Gertie, how she had been  raised by her grandmother...a hundred years older than her, and perhaps that was why Gertie didn't have a typical maternal nature.

Gertie was free-spirited all of her life, and I believe she just did what she wanted to do, as Archie did as well.

This accounts why Dawn was raised by the Winter's family in Prince Albert, and actually spent little time with her parents all together.

Along the shore of Lake Simon while we were there: *"This moment was the closest I had ever been to both of my parents at the same time. I was feeling sorry that some time had not been given to us to be together. I feel an overwhelming joy because I have been to Lake Simon.*

*We went out on Lake Simon in our canoe, and Bob took several pictures. The area is beautiful from the lake. The trees grow almost to the water's edge, and rocks varying in size from pebbles to huge boulders line the beaches. There are many water lilies in the bays; the air is hazy and gives a varied dimensional depth to the islands. Nine children invaded our van, scrambling through the sink, digging out biscuits, donuts and part-loaf of bread, then ran away laughing."*

*"These young boys helped Bob load our canoe, after having their picture taken with some sitting in the canoe, and others standing beside it, before we loaded it on top of our van."*

Dawn and I left Lake Simon the next day, back-tracked to the Noranda area, then down highway 101 to highway 11, and headed for Temagami.

We reached Lake Temagami in the evening, and went straight to the Provincial Park and set up camp for the night. We recognized we were in Grey Owl Country again. Dawn smiled when she noticed the plaque in the Park honouring her father.

The first morning in Temagami we took a water-taxi to Bear Island, and met Chief Gary Potts` son Rick, and the Band Lawyer, Bruce Clark. In Dawn`s journal she writes: *"Showed Rick Potts my birth certificate , and he was very interested in my name being Grey Owl. He showed us the hand-hewn library building, which unfortunately was now covered with siding on the exterior. The inside, however, the hewn logs were still exposed. There was a sketch on the wall of my father with the notation, this was the building in which Archie and Angele were married. I also saw a book `Northern Faces', where the author said they had married on the Temagami Belle, and that it was just a drunken brawl. Later, I mentioned it to Gary Pots, the Chief, and he said they were accustomed to stories like that...and didn`t know the truth of it."*

*"The houses on the Island were scattered. The island had a shore line of six miles around it. There were between 125 and 175 people on the Reserve. We met a beautiful little girl, four years old with big brown almond-shaped eyes, and her name was Manda. Bob took a picture of the girl with Gramma Katt, and another picture of her standing by a big tree just before we left. We stopped for lunch on the veranda of the dance hall. The whole area plays Grey Owl up to the hilt."*

Dawn was pleased with our journey to Bear Island; a
warm welcome. It eliminated any traces of the
apprehension Dawn had been feeling before our arrival

While we were on the Island we met an older Indian,
George. He told us bluntly, "$16.00 is too much to pay for
water taxi," and he took us back to the mainland. Dawn
insisted that he take the money for the ride, and he
eventually accepted it hesitantly, gracefully. It was a very
exciting day for us to see where her father spent his
first years with the Indians in the wilderness of Northern
Ontario, and to watch Dawn be recognized as
Grey Owl`s daughter . The next day we visited Camp
Wabikon, despite the light rain.

From Dawn`s journal:
*"Bob and I walked along a pathway which followed the
shoreline. There are small, old cabins where young
people stay in an organized camp situation. There is
another book being written. I gather it will be about
Wabikon in the 1940`s. We walked back into the bush a
short way where there were two large wooden structures,
which had been there during the time of my parents."*

There were a group of young people at Camp Wabikon
while we were there, and Dawn was introduced to the
group and invited to share her reminiscences. As she
spoke about her father, I could see her pride in Grey Owl,
and they listened with great interest. She enjoyed talking
with the group,  being able to speak about her

parents, especially in this memorable place Camp Wabikon where Archie had first met Anahareo.

When we left the Temagami area we drove south to North Bay, then highway 17 to Mattawa, where Gertie was born and raised. Arriving Mattawa, we drove around the small town. Later, Dawn finally met Gertie's family, the many relatives and friends of Gertie's family, including her older sister of ten years. She also met Gertie's older brother Fred. What a warm reception we got in Mattawa! We were invited to stay, so we did for a couple of nights. Dawn had never met some of the younger relatives of her mother, and she was happy to meet her mother's older sister again.

We attended a concert on one evening. It was old-time fiddling and step-dancing contest. It was an interesting performance for us to see, quite different than anything we saw in our Kamloops neighbourhood. After we left the Mattawa area we headed to Cabano, Quebec and the Birch Lake area; an important stop. This is the McGinty and McInnis area, the two Macs often referred to by both Archie and Anahareo. These were their first two beavers who were little kits.

We travelled along the North side of the St. Lawrence River from Montreal eastward, stopping in Quebec City briefly to visit The Plains of Abraham. Then we continued on to Ste. Simeon, taking the Ferry across the St. Lawrence to Riviere du-Loop. Upon our arrival at Cabano we camped in the Municipal Campground.

Cabano is along the shore of Lake Temiscouata, another area Gertie had talked about a lot. She and Archie had seen Elephant Mountain across the lake from Cabano. Then beyond the mountain they had hiked in to Birch Lake. It was while they were in this area that Archie finally gave up trapping. It was also where he and Gertie nurtured the two beaver kits McGinty and McGinnis.

Previous to our arrival there, Dawn had contacted a Mrs. Berube who had replied saying that a reception was being planned, as Grey Owl and Anahareo were held in high esteem throughout the area. *"The reception was unbelievable"*, Dawn states in her journal. *"The Mayor, an Alderman, and an interpreter arrived at the Campground. The Mayor was Mrs. Nicol, and we were immediately invited to the Town Hall for a drink, and to meet with other Aldermen. Mrs. Berube and her son Peter also arrived. Mrs. Berube, I believe, was not accustomed to such austere company. The people headed straight for me as if greeting an old friend."*

Mrs. Berube, a quite elderly woman, who had known both Archie and Gertie well, insisted that we later go to her home and see where Anahareo had slept in 1976, when she came when the town honoured her and Archie. She also wanted to show Dawn where she used to live, where she'd see Archie and Anahareo walking by on their way into town  She showed Dawn where they had beached their canoe.

Mrs. Berube commented: *"Your father was not just a man... he was a gentleman."* This comment pleased Dawn, especially as she had the same remarks from Lottie and Libby Sawyer in Bisco.

Mrs. Nicol and her husband took us for dinner at the nicest restaurant in Cabano, and we continued to learn Dawn's parents were respected by most people there. Dawn comments in her travel journal: *"It is food for thought that there are a few people who are only concerned about who Grey Owl slept with, how many children he fathered, and where he was born."*

It is sad that some people do not give credit where credit is due, but Dawn was happy with our journey, grateful to know that her parents were heroes to most people. The next day we were given a tour of the paper mill and the operations, accompanied by Alfred Caron, a long time resident of Cabano. He had a four-wheel drive vehicle and he agreed to take us to Birch Lake the next day.

Alfred picked us up shortly after eight in the morning, since after leaving the main highway there was still ten miles to travel on old logging roads to Birch Lake. Dawn's journal reads: *" When we arrived close to the lake, the loons greeted us with their call of the wild. It was a small lake, very still and gentle. There are no camps on the lake, and the solitude is beautiful; just as it was when my Mom and Dad were there. Bob picked up three pieces of fungus by the lake, along with a couple of small stones from the shore line. When Alfred got us back to Cabano, he gave Bob a brand new axe handle he had carved himself. Bob got him to write his name on it. It was a thoughtful gift for us."*

While we were in Cabano we were introduced to Roger Roy, who told Dawn that her mother would swim across Lake Temiscouata with a pack on her back. *"She could swim like a fish"*, he recalled. He also told her a story about her mother throwing a knife at a fellow who'd tried to make a pass at her. *"The knife winged by the fellow's ear, less than an inch away. The man left with no further problem."*

This was part of my trip as well as Dawn's. I was invited to show a few of my paintings at their museum with a wine and cheese evening. We met many new friends in Cabano, and the day after this reception we left Cabano and headed for Metis Beach. Metis is on the Gaspe where Archie gave his first lecture in one of the big tourist hotels, almost 55 years prior to our visit.

It rained lightly for most of the travel from Cabano, so when we got to Metis, we realized we were tired and booked into a motel. I didn't feel like setting up camp in the rain and we had reached the final destination. After we rested and had supper, I phoned Audry Astle, as she was interested in talking about Grey Owl and Anahareo with Dawn. She agreed to come over to the motel the next morning.

She took us on a tour to the pond where Grey Owl and Anahareo and Jelly Roll had been camped. Then she showed us the location where two of the big hotels had stood , and where, in one, Archie spoke to the public for the first time. In Archie`s time, there were the "Seaside Hotel ", and "the Hillside Inn". Both hotels overlooked the St. Lawrence and Boule Rock was immediately in front of them. Their only remains we could see were some scattered chunks of concrete along the shore line.

Then we walked through the bushes to the small pond where Dawn`s father and mother had been allowed to set up their camp; exciting and emotional for Dawn, through wet grass and small dripping bushes. It had been a farm when Dawn`s parents were there. Circling the pond were red willow and some small maple and poplars. Apparently the pond had been much larger back then, and had been stocked with fish.

Audry pointed out a second pond where Dawn`s parents had tented with Jelly Roll. The pond was very small, and had diminished in size because of the highway construction. Both ponds were fed by a small stream, and would have been ideal for beaver as the St. Lawrence was salt water at this point. We took some photos then Audry invited us to her home where we were joined by Ruby and Doris, who had visited Anahareo almost everyday when she`d lived in this area.They told us that Grey Owl and Anahareo had spent the entire summer at Metis Beach, lecturing at the hotels, and both were equally appreciated by the tourists.

In six weeks we had travelled 5460 miles, and now we were again heading west going home. Along the way we

continued touring and stopped at the Konawaski Reserve.
Then we crossed the Ottawa River
by ferry to Oka. The lands at Oka are under the
sovereignty of the Mohawk people, and they hope to
maintain the beauty of the land for future generations.

We also visited Kenesatke Reserve, and enjoyed chatting
with Ron Bonspeil, an interesting, small chunky man. He
told us that there were between 850 and 900 people on the
Reserve who can buy and sell their houses amongst
themselves.

Dawn and I were impressed with their Cultural Centre.
Ron explained: *"Indians don`t want to have their children
go to school off the Reserve. They will lose their desire to
be Indians. We have fought the Federal Government to
prevent amalgamation."* We listened to
Ron`s philosophy: *"An Indian should not have to pay
taxes on or off the Reserve."* He believes an Indian is an
Indian, no matter where he is.

Soon after talking with Ron we left on our journey
westward again. Along the highway we came to a
beautiful home that was advertising Maple Syrup for sale.
Dawn wanted to buy maple candy for her old friend Mrs.
Winters, so we turned into the home in the grove of maple
trees.

A buxom lady with greying hair greeted us most cordially,
inviting us into her house to taste her syrup.
She proudly showed us through the house explaining that
she and her husband designed it. She was a warm, gentle

person like most French we'd met. Visiting with her reminded us how we'd like to visit Quebec again. We loved visiting Quebec and hoped to be able to do it again some day.

Both of us had gained much from this trip. I had done a lot of sketching and taken a lot of photos throughout the Grey Owl areas. I planned to portray these places in paintings. As we drove we talked particularly about what we would like to do next year, 1984. Dawn was happy.
Our travels had enabled her to visit many of the places where her father and mother had lived.

We realized that one major place in the world for her still to see was Hastings, England, her father's birthplace. Hastings was where Archie Belaney had lived and been educated by his two spinster aunts. We both kept thinking about what would we do for 1984.

# 109

Chapter 6

We decided as Dawn and I talked, about creating a series of paintings titled: *"Images of Grey Owl and Anahareo's Wilderness"*. Dawn would write to Hastings expressing our wishes to visit her father's birthplace, and mentioning that she could also be a part of a show exhibiting personal family photos and some of my art work.

When we arrived back in B.C., we travelled straight through to Vancouver to visit with Leonard and Florence before returning to our mountain home for the winter. We spent three days with them. Our photos provoked some interesting conversation with Leonard about Moosonee and Moose Factory. From the time Leonard had been stationed there with the Hudson Bay Company, half a century had separated our visit. Before we left we told them what our proposed agenda was for our next trip in 1984. Then we started for home, already planning our next journey.

After travelling for over two months it took us a few days to settle in. We had experienced a journey which gave us memories of a lifetime. The first evening at home, I made a bonfire in the firepit of our yard and we sat by it with our brandy and coffee.

We started planning for 1984. Dawn wrote to the Mayor of Hastings, who in turn sent Dawn's letter to Victoria Williams, Curator of the Hastings Museum and Gallery. We received an answer in less than a month. Both the Mayor and Victoria Williams warmly accepted our proposed visit to Hastings. They wrote that they would like to plan a reception and they would appreciate knowing the date of our arrival, as well as how many works we would be bringing with us for display.

After another letter to Hastings Museum and Gallery, our opening was set for May 26, 1984, and available for public viewing until June 17th. The Exhibition would be assisted through the efforts of the newly formed Grey Owl Society, which conveniently was based in Hastings.

Dawn and I were pleased to be invited and she was looking forward to visiting the city of her father's birth. We realized we needed to get to work. I jotted down a number of ideas for painting compositions complimentary to our Canadian travels, and to the places where Grey Owl and Anahareo had lived and travelled.

Dawn was revising her manuscript SMOKE. I started painting as I wanted to have thirty completed. As well, I was searching for an appropriate publisher for Dawn's book. November and December passed quickly.

In Kamloops one January day, we spotted a 1976 Winnebago motor home on one of the auto lots. It was in beautiful condition with only twenty-five thousand miles on the odometer. We made an offer to purchase. Two days later we were the proud owners of the Winnebago, having decided to sell our Dodge van in the spring. As the snow piled up around our mountain home, and we looked out through the upstairs window of our studio, we recognized our tranquility. We watched the Whiskey Jacks and Steller`s Jays flutter from tree to tree, dodging a big squirrel who seemed to be demanding sole occupancy of the territory. Some mornings if I had failed to put goodies out for them, the Steller`s Jays would peck on the dining room window.Dawn and I were extremely happy and content, sometimes working, other times just sitting by the big wood stove contemplating the year to come.

At the end of January we went to Vancouver with the landcruiser to visit Leonard and Florence, feeling ready for a break as we`d both been working hard. We were welcomed warmly , as usual. We enjoyed three days of chatting, combined with short walks over to Oakridge Mall, where Dawn would find treats for Leonard and Florence, things like candies or cream puffs. Florence was an early riser, so she would go to bed early, and Leonard would chat with us to the late news, or even later. He was always interested in Dawn`s activities, just as a father would be.

In his seventies by this time, Leonard was still working as administrator for the Canadian Legion Poppy Fund. He told us how he helped the needs of some of the vets with temporary help, a few having financial or medical needs. He liked to recall his time in the British army, being in the Occupation Forces in Europe before coming to Canada in 1950. They had no children, although Florence had two sons from a previos marriage, Paul and Maurice. Maurice lived in the Seattle area and

Paul was an English teacher at the University of Edinburgh, Scotland. Leonard, Paul and Morag, his wife, and their three children had spent five days with us at Knouff Lake. They enjoyed being driven in our wilderness and fishing on the small lakes. After Paul and Leonard canoed for the day, we all enjoyed a bonfire at the lake, especially purcolating the coffee over the open fire.

By March, Dawn and I had accomplished much work. Dawn had completed revising her manuscript SMOKE, and I had only a few more paintings to finish. For a short break we took a trip to Spokane in our Winnebago, thoroughly enjoying our two days spent in Spokane. When we arrived back home again we were ready to finish our preparations for England.

For Dawn's book, I searched for a publisher who liked Aboriginal themes and wilderness living. I found one in the Kapuskasing area in Ontario. I carefully drafted a query letter, bundled up the manuscript and sent it off, then awaited their response feeling positive. Meanwhile, I completed a few more paintings and had all of them on stretched canvases. Now I could count thirty which could be used in the British Exhibition in Hastings. We were ready.

Framing the paintings was not feasible so I finished the edges with presentable plastic mouldings. Then I built plywood containers. Thirty fit in two protective containers which stacked neatly, allowing us to take them as excess baggage.

In April, we both were looking forward to our journey to England, and in particular , to Hastings. The time was close when Dawn would finally see the city where her father was born. She would feel the emotions of walking in the city park where her father had played as a child, and she would touch the floors and walls of the room her father had lived and studied in as a youth. This would be a major highlight of her life.

Dawn began having chest pains again. They were not as severe this time, but we immediately consulted her doctor. He believed they were angina symtoms and gave her a prescription for nito-glycerine tablets. They eased her problems and she appeared to be feeling well again.

We phoned England and learned the Opening evening would be co-sponsored by the Grey Owl Society. Everything was fitting nicely into its proper place. We left in our Winnebago near mid May, intending to visit with Leonard and Florence for a few days prior to our departure for England. We were excited and Leonard and Florence were excited for us. The atmosphere was full of positive energy.

On our second morning at Leonard's Dawn began having severe chest pains at 6:00a.m. I took her to St. Paul's where she was admitted immediately. I sat at her bedside bewildered, confused, and questioning myself, as I watched over her while she rested with the help of oxygen.

By 8:00a.m. she was feeling settled again and had no discomfort in her chest. When I arrived back at the home of Leonard and Florence, I told them both what had taken place. Florence, a trained nurse, commented that once Dawn had a few days rest, she would probably be ok to travel.

I knew Dawn was eagerly looking forward to our journey, as I pondered what to do, thinking that perhaps we should delay the trip to England. She told the doctor about our plans; he did not discourage her, as she had another three days to recover before our flight.

Although I was thinking about what to do when Dawn and I talked, we decided to wait another day before changing any travel plans. When I went to the hospital the next morning, Dawn had been taken off oxygen and the colour was back in her cheeks. She was eating well and was able to take short walks around the ward. I felt certain that someone was guiding us; it was meant to be.

We would be able to journey to England as planned. One day before our flight, Dawn was discharged. We sat in the sun in the yard and I realized how much our journey meant to her, and how determined she was to see her father's birth place.

We boarded our flight to England arriving in London on the morning of May 23rd. When it took three hours to clear customs with my paintings there were no serious problems, but it took time to tend to the formalities. We had to wait for a broker to come down to view the works, and we also had to contact Victoria Williams of the Hastings Gallery. Because we were offering the work for sale, it seemed that Customs Officials needed clarification regarding the collection of the VAT on any sales.

In the overcast cool weather we caught a double-decker bus from Heathrow to downtown Victoria Station, then a transit bus to Hastings. By the time we checked in to our seaside hotel, we were both exhausted. I could see Dawn was struggling and again I questioned whether we were doing what was best for her. She was reaching for the nitro- glycerine tablets. After a couple of hours of rest at the hotel she appeared to be feeling quite well again. We had a light dinner in the dining room, then retreated for rest, too tired to contact anyone in Hastings that day.

Dawn rested quite well. After breakfast we caught a taxi to the Museum and Gallery. We met with Curator, Victoria Williams for a short time, to leave our work with her so that staff could mount the displays as they wished. After lunch we contacted the Grey Owl Society, whose representative showed us around town. We stopped in front of the house where Archie had been raised by his two aunts. The residents warmly showed as through the interior, including Grey Owl`s boyhood room. Dawn paused in the silence of the room and smiled at a photograph of her father as a child, then at the other photo beside it showing him in Native Indian head-dress.

She gave a nod, apparently understanding the transition of her father`s life; of the father who had gone from being the little English boy, to North American Indian. She was proud as we left the Historical house. She turned and took one last look at the plaque honouring him; an acknowledgement by the city of Hastings.

Dawn was only five years old when her father died in April 1938. She had often been asked what she remembered about her father, and she`d reply: *"I actually lost him in the publicity and the photos of recognition he had achieved. But I remember the smell of his buck-skins while I sat upon his knee, and the warmth of his hands."*

He had captured audiences throughout the United Kingdom, when people had queued for city blocks to see this Red Skin; this North American Indian in Native Buckskin dress. Sir Richard Attenborough, who sixty years later produced and directed the big screen movie: THE GREY OWL STORY, could remember seeing him as a young boy. No wonder Dawn carried her father`s torch throughout her adult life.

I was proud of her and aware how pleased she was to have the opportunity to follow the footprints of her father. Perhaps she felt she was the part of his final chapter as Conservationist. His message continues to grow with every decade, as we see the pollution and poison spread throughout the Planet. *"We belong to Nature; not it to us,"* she`d say, speaking with the conviction that her father had spoken many years earlier.

On the evening of May 26th, in the Hastings Museum, the Agent-General for Saskatchewan, Mr. R.A. Larter opened our event. The Mayor of Hastings, Councillor Roy Saunders, and representatives from the B.B.C., the Canadian High Commission and the Grey Owl Society were also present. After our introduction, Dawn spoke eloquently to the gathering crowd of people. Then we mingled amongst the guests enjoying the evening and the great dignity Grey Owl`s daughter received.

Our display of art and photos was popular, and was to be available for the public to view from May 26th to June 17th, 1984. Over three-thousand people passed through our Exhibition, viewing the displays we had brought from Canada.

It was late in the evening when we returned to our hotel to rest again, and to prepare for the following day. Dawn was to be interviewed by a lady from the B.B.C. Radio in the morning, and then she was to appear at the Hastings Museum in the afternoon for B.B.C. Television interview.

During the TV interview, as Grey Owl had lectured and entertained the Royal Family in Buckingham Palace, the interviewer turned to Dawn and abruptly asked her:

*"Why did your father deceive the King and Royal
Family?"*

Dawn answered with her usual diplomacy:
*"I believe my father had the heart and soul of an Indian,
and the strength of character of the British people."*
She had always been diplomatic, particularly when
dealing with questionable criticisms of her father, always
capable of helping people understand.

She was convinced about her father`s philosophy, and that
he had done important work helping to protect and value
our Canadian wilderness. As we see the condition
of our planet at the turn of this new century, we cannot
help believe that Grey Owl was far ahead of his time, and
that we need to ask ourselves: What are we doing with
our planet now?

Dawn was not feeling well again the next morning, and
was needing to take more nitro-glycerine tablets. Yet at
that point in time I wasn`t too concerned. I totally
believed she would bounce back to being her normal self
again, as she had done so many times before. and that it
was the stress of this journey that was affecting her.

After lunch we walked to the White Rock Pavilion
where her father had spoken. We entered the silent
building and she stood beside me viewing the huge stage
area. The stage area was in total darkness, and I`m sure
she could visualize her father standing alone on the
centre-stage in full Indian Chief head-dress, with the spot
light coming down upon him as he spoke: *"You are tired*

*of years of civilization ....I bring you a single green leaf."*

She heard his voice echo across the passing half a century. Again I saw a tear on her cheek, and I knew this was the major event of her life; coming to England to her father's birth place, allowed her to sense her father by her side once again.

We sauntered along the ocean front in the afternoon, then rested on the wharf and talked about taking a trip across the English Channel to France. We decided we could go over there and rest for a few days. Dawn was weary from all the activities, and we needed a few days to ourselves to relax.

We walked leisurely through the Hastings Park that afternoon following the footprints of her father, in solitude together. Dawn was tired and as we paused briefly for a rest, she commented:
*"Wouldn't it be strange, if I died in the city my father was born in?"*

She wasn't feeling well, and I knew it, as she had been taking more nitro-glycerine tablets. We went back to our hotel for an early rest before going to the Taylor's that evening for tea.

A short time after we'd arrived at the Taylor's I noticed Dawn's complexion change. She was having difficulty. Her chest pains were getting stronger. Our host phoned a doctor who arrived quickly and suggested that Dawn should be hospitalized. She was admitted to St. Helen's hospital. I sat with her until midnight; she was on oxygen. When she was finally free of chest pains and dozing off to sleep. I left for the hotel letting her know that I would be back in the morning.

When I arrived at the hospital the next morning, she appeared to be doing well on intravenous, comfortable and talkative. We discussed going to Scotland, to Edinburgh when she'd recovered, planning that we could spend time at Leonard's step-son's home resting leisurely.

Then on June 17th, we'd return to Hastings to pack our works, express our thanks and say farewell to the people of Hastings for a warm and cordial reception. I knew Dawn had always bounced back from these incidents and I was sure, that once we arrived back at Knouff Lake, all would be well again.

I sat with Dawn day and night over the next few days as her condition worsened; in addition to the heart problems, her kidneys were failing. The hospital staff ordered me a couch in an adjoining room of the visitors area, but I couldn't sleep. I stayed with Dawn beside her bed.

The hospital in Hastings had no dialysis, so the doctor made arrangements for Dawn's transport to London. I was told to be ready to leave within the hour. Will and Angela Kelleher of the Grey Owl Society took all of our baggage in their car, and followed the ambulance to

Guy`s Hospital in London. I was grateful for them being with us and for their assistance. I was completely exhausted from the days and nights in St. Helens, worried and deeply apprehensive.

As I`d seen Dawn pull through illness in the past, I still held some hope that she would be allright, once she was on dialysis. We arrived Guy`s Hospital about two hours after leaving Hastings, and the Emergency staff wasted no time transferring her to the renal ward. She was on the dialysis machine within thirty minutes.

It was a time for waiting, waiting and waiting. When I went into the renal room, Dawn was only half alert, and I sat quietly at her bedside. I held her hand, hoping and praying that all would be well. I was told she would be on dialysis for four hours, then she would be transferred to Intensive Care. The comment she made while we were slowly strolling in the Hastings City Park, haunted my thoughts as I sat beside her.

When the four hours was almost up, Dawn was quite alert, her colour had improved and her speech was lucid. She knew where she was and what was taking place. I kissed her forehead and told her I would go down to the cafeteria and have a sandwich. I would meet her in Intensive Care when I came back upstairs. I touched her hand, kissed her forehead again and left.

That was my last touch of my Dawn. It was June 3rd, 1984. When I returned upstairs I was told she passed away immediately after the shutting down of the dialysis.

Her heart was tired, and she died close to the city where her father was born. I have recalled her comment again and again: *"Wouldn't it be strange if I died in the city where my father was born."*

Sadly, premonition became true. Even though we had made the journey she had longed for all of her adult life, I was now without her, crying in the silence, knowing Dawn had been born in Prince Albert, Saskatchewan, and died in England; her father was born in England and died in Prince Albert .

The circle was complete.

The End

## The Epilogue

Five days later, I arrived at our empty house on the mountain at Knouff Lake, more exhausted and stressed than I had ever experienced in my life. Local arrangements for a Memorial Service had to be made. Then I would travel again to Beaver Lodge, Lake Ajawaan, where Dawn would finally be at peace along with her father.

She was more than my wife; she was my best friend and spiritual partner. We'd lost an Historical person. People continually phoned from London, Hastings and Canadian cities. I picked up our mail from the Heffley Creek Post Office, and there was one letter which caught my immediate interest. It was a letter from the Ontario Publisher, saying they wanted to publish Dawn's book, SMOKE. I then disclosed her background as we had previously arranged. She had wanted her book accepted on its merits, not because she was the daughter of Grey Owl and Anahareo.

I felt so proud of her, knowing that she would be smiling from *"the other side."* I then made arrangements to do small charcoal illustrations for her book.

Following Dawn's Memorial Service, I climbed into our Winnebago and headed east. With me, were Dawn's two children and my brother. When we arrived at Waskesiu, Saskatchewan, Parks Canada, Merv Syroteuk and staff, took us by power boat across Kingsmere Lake.

We walked the two miles up the quiet pathway to Lake Ajawaan and Beaver Lodge. On the knoll overlooking the lake and cabin, and close to her father's grave, I gently placed Dawn in her final resting place.

As I looked out across the lake beyond the stillness of the cabin where she had romped and played as a child, with Jelly Roll and Rawhide, I visualized the two beavers swimming towards the shore to welcome her, while Grey Owl and Anahareo stood watching by the cabin.

On my return to our empty home on the mountain, I built a small fire within the circle of stones and sat gazing into the flames. We'd enjoyed great conversation and laughter by this fire. But now, as the burning embers died, I felt more lonely than I had ever felt in my life, missing Dawn.

In the years since, I still miss her. What adventures we had. With every Steller's Jay or squirrel I see she's nearby me, teaching folks about our Environment and Conservation. I think Dawn would say as her father did before her:

*"We belong to Nature; not it to us."*

\*\*\*\*\*\*\*\*\*\*\*\*

ISBN 155212719-2